An Illustrated Introduction to
Classical Horsemanship

Concepts and Skills from A to Z

Second Edition

A comprehensive resource in a succinct alphabetical format that brings the beginning rider through every aspect of learning to train and ride for show and trail with over one hundred detailed explanations and eighty illustrations and photos that organize and clarify the most important concepts for beginning riders and trainers—a concise and easy to use reference guide to beginning horsemanship with an introductory chapter on establishing an attitude toward riding with which you will exceed your best performance—by an internationally known authority on performance training and assessment.

Gary D. Borich

An Illustrated Introduction to Classical Horsemanship:
Concepts and Skills from A to Z

Gary D. Borich

A Leading Rein Publication
Thousand Oaks, California

Second Edition
Copyright © 2011 by Gary D. Borich

All Rights Reserved. No part of this book may be reproduced or transmitted by any means, electronic or mechanical including photocopying, recording or by any information or storage and retrieval system, without written permission from the author, except for brief quotations embodied in critical articles or reviews.

The author is not liable for any property damage or damages arising from the injury or death of a participant or spectator resulting from the content contained in this book. Each participant in an equine activity expressly assumes the risk and legal responsibility for any property damage or damages arising from the personal injury or death that results from the inherent risk of equine activities. It is the duty of each participant to act within the limits of the participant's own ability, to maintain reasonable control of the particular equine at all times while participating in an equine activity, to heed all warning and to refrain from acting in a manner that may cause or contribute to the injury of any person or damage to property.

ISBN: 978-1-257-10231-0

About the Author

An internationally known authority on training and performance assessment, Gary D. Borich is Professor in the Department of Educational Psychology and a Cissy McDaniel Parker Endowed Fellow at The University of Texas at Austin. He is author of 13 books on training and performance assessment, including *Effective Teaching Methods* and *Performance Assessment* and has served as a performance training and assessment consultant to industry and education in the U.S., China, Singapore, India, Germany, Switzerland and the United Arab Emirates. In this book he combines his experience as a participant in the Judges and Exhibitors School of a major international horse association and his love of riding with more than 25 years of experience in performance training and assessment to create a practical reference for the beginning rider and equestrian competitor.

Author with Alazun Ligero.

Author on Heart of Gold.
Scottsdale Top Ten Champion, Hunter Pleasure.

Credits

Cover and book design by **Julian Chapa** (julian.chapa@gmail.com).

Figure illustrations sketched by **Emily Jo Cureton**: 1, 7, 9–10, 13–14, 18, 21–27, 29–30, 41.

Figure illustrations sketched by **David Tenorio**: 2–6, 8, 11–12, 15–17, 19–20, 28, 31–40, 42–44.

Contents

About the Author iii
Table of Figures ix
Table of Photographs xi
Preface xiii
Exceeding Your Best Performance 1
Concepts and Skills from A to Z 9
    Introduction 9
    Above and Behind the Bit 10
    Backing 10
    Balance 11
    Bearing (neck) Rein 11
    Behind the Bit 11
    Bending, in circle and serpentine 11
    Bending, in a corner 12
    Bitting 12
    Bolting 14
    Bradoon 14
    Bucking 14
    Cadence 15
    Canter Depart, methods for 15
    Canter Depart, problems and remedies 18
    Canter, extended and collected 21
    Canter, slowing 22
    Capriole 22
    Cavesson 23
    Centerline 23
    Change of Diagonals (Reins) 23
    Change of Lead, simple 24

Contents

Change of Reins	25
Chin (Lip) Strap	25
Collection	25
Counter Canter	25
Croup (Topline)	26
Curb Chain	26
Diagonal Aids	26
Diagonals	26
Direct Rein	26
Double Bridle	27
Dressage, arena	28
Dressage, definition	28
Dressage, exercise patterns	28
Dressage, levels of	29
Ears, movement of	31
Extension	31
Eyes, rider's	31
FEI (Fédération Equestre Internationale)	32
Flexion	32
Flying Change of Lead	33
Flying Change of Lead, problems and remedies	35
Forehands (Forelegs)	36
Gaits	36
Gallop, hand and full	39
Half-halt	40
Half-pass	40
Halts	40
Hand Gallop	41
Hands, placement of	41
Hand, measure of a horse's height	41
Haunches (hindquarters)	42
Haunches-in/out	42
Head, lowering or raising of	44
Head, proper position of	44
Hocks, cow and bowed	45
Holding (supporting) Leg	45

Contents

Holding (supporting) Rein	45
Hunter Equitation, some tests of performance	46
Impulsion	46
Indirect Rein	47
Inside versus Outside	47
Lateral Aids	47
Lateral Work	48
Leading (open) Rein	48
Leads	48
Leg Aids	48
Leg-yielding	49
Lengthening of Stride	49
Levade	50
Lifting Hand	50
Lunging	51
Lunging, at the canter	51
Mount/dismount	52
Mounting, problems and remedies	54
Neck Rein	54
On the Bit	54
Pace	55
Passage	55
Passive (holding) Rein	55
Piaffe	55
Pirouette	55
Posting	56
Rearing	56
Rein Aids	57
Rein-back	58
Rewarding the Horse	59
Rhythm	59
Riding with Extension	60
Riding with the Motion	60
Rollback	60
Saddle Language	61
Saddle Types	62

Contents

    Seat and Posture, correct 64
    Serpentine, at trot and canter 66
    Setting the Head 66
    Shoulder-in at Halt, Walk and Trot 66
    Shying 67
    Side Pass, half and true 68
    Side Reins 70
    Sitting Trot 70
    Snaffle Bit 70
    Spanish Riding School (Spanische Hofreitschule) 71
    Spurs, correct use of 72
    Squeezing Up 73
    Stirrups, drop and pickup 73
    Stirrups, riding without 73
    Surcingle 74
    Suspension 74
    Top Line 75
    Transitions 75
    Trot (working, collected, extended) 75
    Turn/half-turn on Forehand at Halt 78
    Turn/half-turn on Haunches at Halt 79
    Two and Three-point Position 80
    Two Tracking 82
    Unilateral Half-halt 82
    The Vertical 83
    Voice Commands 83
    Volte 83
    Weight, rider's as an aid 83
    Whips 84
    Yielding Rein 84
    Zenophon 85
Appendix A: List of Quick Cue Notes 87
Appendix B: Eighteen Essential Movements to Good Riding 89

Table of Figures

Figure 1. Above and Behind the Bit 10
Figure 2. Bending, in a circle and serpentine 11
Figure 3. Bending, in a corner 12
Figure 4. Bitting 13
Figure 5. Bradoon 14
Figure 6. Bucking 14
Figure 7. Cavesson 23
Figure 8. Change of Diagonals (Reins) 23
Figure 9. Change of Lead, simple 24
Figure 10. Collection 25
Figure 11. Counter Canter 25
Figure 12. Croup (Topline) 26
Figure 13. Curb Chain 26
Figure 14. Double Bridle 27
Figure 15. Dressage, arena 28
Figure 16. Extension 31
Figure 17. Flying Change of Lead 33
Figure 18. Gaits 36
Figure 19. Hands, placement of 41
Figure 20. Haunches-in/out 42
Figure 21. Head, proper position of 44
Figure 22. Hocks, cow 45
Figure 23. Lengthening of Stride 49
Figure 24. Levade 50
Figure 25. Lunging 51
Figure 26. Passage 55
Figure 27. Piaffe 55
Figure 28. Rearing 56

Table of Figures

Figure 29. Saddle Language 61
Figure 30. Seat and Posture, correct 64
Figure 31. Serpentine, at trot and canter 66
Figure 32. Setting the Head 66
Figure 33. Shoulder-in at Halt, Walk, Trot 67
Figure 34. Shying 67
Figure 35. Side Pass, half and true 68
Figure 36. Side Reins 70
Figure 37. Trot 75
Figure 38. Turn/half-turn on Forehand at Halt 78
Figure 39. Turn/half-turn on Haunches at Halt 79
Figure 40. Two-point Position 80
Figure 41. Two Tracking 82
Figure 42. The Vertical 83
Figure 43. Volte 83
Figure 44. Whips 84

Table of Photographs

Above the Bit	10
Bending, in the corner	12
Bitting, snaffle bridle	13
Canter Depart	16
Canter, collected	21
Capriole	22
Double Bridle	27
Extension	31
Flexion	33
Flying Change of Lead	34
Gaits, working trot	37
Gaits, collected at trot	38
Gaits, at canter	39
Hands, proper position of	41
Haunches-in	43
Head, proper position of	44
Hocks	45
Lengthening of Stride	50
Lunging, at the trot	52
Mount/dismount series	53
Piaffe	56
Rearing	57
Rein-back	59
Riding with Extension	60
Saddle Types, close contact	63
Saddle Types, dressage	63
Seat and Posture, correct alignment	65
Seat and Posture, proper heels down position	65

Table of Photographs

Side Pass, half-pass to the left 68
Spanish Riding School, inside the Grand Arena 71
Spur 72
Stirrups, riding without 74
Trot, working 76
Trot, collected 77
Trot, extended 77
Turn on Forehand, to the left 79
Two-point Position 81

Preface

Most beginning riders have read about horsemanship long before they have ever sat on their first horse. And, if you are like most new riders, young or old, you soon want to learn more, to ride better and to move up to more challenging horses that require not only better horsemanship but also the knowledge to train them to perform as you wish. As a rider, trainer and professor of educational psychology at the University of Texas at Austin for 25 years, I have read many books on horsemanship to improve my skills and have been witness to the difficulty of transferring what I have read to the arena or on the trail. This was not the fault of the authors of the books I had read, most of whom had impressive records of accomplishments and national and international championships to their credit. It comes from a different source.

In my professional life, when I'm not in the saddle, I study why people learn some things and why they don't learn others. And, I have come to the conclusion that writing for others to acquire knowledge is very different from writing for others to apply what they have read. It is in fact why we sometimes can do so well on a test and then fail to make sense of what we have learned in the real world. There is many a slip between the cup and the lip—and between learning something and being able to apply it. For lawyers, teachers, physicians, engineers, and symphony conductors, knowledge about something cannot be separated from the ability to apply that knowledge. Some books do a better job at erasing the distinction than others, but when all is read and done, many young riders are left without the skill to directly transfer what was read to the arena and trail. Frustrated by this "disconnect" over the years, I began slowly to untangle "knowledge" from "performance," often

Preface

stopping my horse in "midstream" and on bits of paper tucked in my back pocket converting key bits of knowledge about riding and training I had learned from the great masters on horsemanship into a language that could be easily interpreted by riders of all ages and experience. I then used what I had written in my own riding in the practice arena and on the trail to check if I had translated the wisdom of the great horsemen correctly—and that it could be applied by a beginning rider. Therefore, I have directed this book to beginning riders who want the valued insights of the great horsemen in a single resource, but who also want to immediately apply those insights to their own horsemanship skills without always having the benefit of an experienced rider or professional trainer close at hand to interpret what they have read.

Therefore, I have placed the concepts and skills that are indispensable to all good riding and training in a format that is accessible to the beginning rider and amateur trainer. My task was to condense the wisdom of classical horsemanship into words and illustrations that could be applied by readers of all ages to help them to become better riders and to deal with the questions and problems that naturally arise as they seek to better themselves as their experience and love of riding grows. The carefully crafted explanations, detailed illustrations and photos in this book become a practical tool for reaching this goal. Finally, it is important to note that there are many movements in classical horsemanship that can be executed in several equally effective ways. For purposes of this book, I have chosen those that are easier for the beginning rider, although not always offering the same level of precision that might expected of a more advanced rider.

There are two ways you can use this book, and I hope you will discover this book with them both. The first is to read each entry from A to Z, as you would a book, after introducing yourself to the 10 basic concepts and skills essential to all forms of riding and exhibition that I introduce at the beginning of this book. The entries that follow are in alphabetical order for ease of access and cross-reference. Concepts listed elsewhere in the text used in the process of describing an entry have been placed in italics for easy

Preface

look up. These related concepts in italics will encourage you to move back and forth among entries increasing your vocabulary and knowledge as needed. Your knowledge and the ability to apply it will grow incrementally as you finish reading one entry and go on to the next. You will also benefit from just the right amount of repetition and interrelatedness to give you the details in ways that are connected to the big picture of what good riding is.

This book also includes some special features that help you quickly to transfer your knowledge to the arena and on the trail. A feature called *Quick Cue Note* at the end of selected entries summarizes the sequence of cues required to execute basic movements required for the beginning levels of dressage, other competitive show classes and on the trail. These cues appear again in Appendix A as a list providing a one-stop at-a-glance summary of how to cue your horse for all basic movements. In addition, Appendix B includes a self-checklist of movements for dressage, Training Level through Level 3, that will enable you to keep a running record of your practice sessions and the progress you are making on a scale from 0, "haven't tried it yet" to 4, "have it nailed." This checklist will also acquaint you with some of the most important movements and patterns required in the beginning levels of dressage, in showing and on the trail.

After spending the few hours it will take you to read the entries in this book, you will then have a ready reference you can return to for much of what you have learned from your instructor, other books and videos to be a good rider and trainer at the beginning levels of dressage, exhibition in the show ring, and on the trail. It is then that you will want to return to this book's convenient alphabetical listings to give you access to what your instructor and the masters have said in a form that you can apply to your own riding at the moment you need it. May it serve you well as a reference, an inspiration and an introduction to classical horsemanship.

GDB
Austin, Texas
GaryBorich@mail.utexas.edu

Author on board American Exchange.

Exceeding Your Best Performance

Before reading about the concepts and skills of good riding that follow, let's consider one of the most important facets of good riding—your attitude. Books and videos focus on the techniques of training and how to ride. But, while those techniques and skills will be the foundation of your efforts to train and ride, they cannot be effective without the right attitude with which you approach the learning of those skills. As any horseperson knows, training and riding are not concepts to be taught as much as they are skills that must be acquired. They require the practice of split second decisions and the ability to change what you are doing influenced by the behavior of your horse and the conditions before you. No book or video can reproduce this real-world environment.

Attention to Attitude

No matter what phase of training or riding you are in, attention to your attitude must come first. The confidence and calmness with which you approach your training and riding can make the difference whether or not you are in control of what you want you and your horse to do. Since no one can learn to ride without being on a horse, you'll quickly find that things not always go as books portray. Decisions to do this or do that often emerge without you having the luxury to anticipate them. This is where your attitude can make the difference whether you remain calm and collected, miss opportunities to change things for the better or "mess things up" more. But, what is the proper "attitude." After all, it's not as though you can touch it or put it in a bottle for when you need it.

Body, Breath and Mind

Our mind, like an unruly ill-tempered horse, is difficult to control, especially under stress or unexpected challenges. Like an untamed horse trampling through the field, your mind, not just your horse, must be controlled and disciplined. And, like your horse only when it is calm and gentle can it respond to your wishes. To acquire the proper attitude, three things have to be regulated and in focus: your body, your breath, and your mind. The body has to be steady and upright, comfortable and calm, without moving unintentionally and without any feeling of stress and tension. The eyes are alert and your mouth is closed. And, you must regulate your breathing until the inhalations and exhalations gradually become softer and longer, as if there were no breathing at all.

When the mind is concentrated and composed, your posture will naturally become secure and steady also. When the mind is master, the body is in a state of stillness. Then, as the mind and breath are mutually dependent, you can reach a state of concentration from which your speed of learning and your reaction to events before you will noticeably improve. Your mind overrides the body and now anything is possible—if you put your mind to it.

Concentration

As you have noticed in life, when under stress you lack concentration and your ability to respond and learn from a situation is diminished. But, the good part is that your attitude controls your mind, not the other way around. That ability was there all the time, in your mind, waiting to be unleashed by your attitude. Here are a few suggestions from good riders who have used their attitude, sometimes over their physical skill, to achieve extraordinary feats in performance, dressage, endurance, and jumping. These suggestions comprise the essence of what practical experience and books tell us about how you can exceed your best performance in the arena and on the trail. Our overall plan for your best performance will be to break the bonds of your self-imposed but often unconscious limitations. This plan has several simple components about which you already know something about.

Self 1

Much of what we fail to do or to accomplish is the result of the interference between two contradictory parts of ourselves that we will call Self 1 and Self 2. Self 1 is that part of you that you use when you are consciously thinking, remembering facts, trying to solve a problem, or judging the accuracy of things, just as in school when you try to figure out if you did things well enough to get a good grade from the teacher. Since we all have egos, Self 1 is constantly working to see if our performance measures up to what others expect. Self 1's judgments are based not only on the criteria of performance taught to us in school, but also on standards that are accumulated throughout life as to what others might expect (parents, friends, coach and trainer). One might think of Self 1 as our thinking self or schoolhouse self, although we use this part of us in almost every context, some far removed from the classroom, such as learning to ride.

Self 2

Self 2 is quite a different part of ourselves. Self 2 represents our performing self as opposed to our thinking self. It is Self 2 that guides us through the early stages of learning to walk or to ride a bike. If you think about it, oral directions or written instructions had little to do in acquiring these skills. Those who begin riding at a very early age also depend almost entirely on Self 2. Their bodies quickly acquire a natural and efficient posture without having to look at a diagram or repeat what the instructor has said. But strangely enough, Self 2 is often the least influential but most needed side of us. It is the least influential in that as we grow older it is frequently restrained by Self 1, and it is the most needed in that it is what directs our performance in the real world. This lopsided arrangement is one of the reasons we have so much difficultly putting into practice what we already know and it is often the reason for our disappointment in not performing as well as we would have liked.

The Importance of Context

The mind is a wonderful and complicated instrument. Unfortunately, it is not sufficient to get us through the tangle of decision-making settings in which most riders find themselves.

I have often observed the effect of Self 1 in the actions of beginning riders. They are confronted with an unexpected decision to which they know they must respond, so Self 1 goes to work, rapidly sorting through the knowledge that they may have been taught or acquired from experience. Self 1 finds the best match possible and gives the command to Self 2 for execution, all in a matter of seconds. In the few seconds Self 1 is searching, a sense of uncertainty comes over the beginning rider. Then, having come up with an idea of what to do, the decision is executed by Self 2 and the rider is noticeably relieved that this situation is over.

What the rider does not notice, however, is that he or she was capable of a better or more graceful response that was more attuned to the situation and, in fact, may have given that response before when the situation was not as tense and demanding. In other words, had this rider not thought about it so much, the response that was needed would have come naturally without the interference of Self 1. It is as though all the information ever read or told to you relevant to the problem at hand was consulted in a flash. The result often is not a bad response, but neither is it a response that the situation requires and of which you are capable of performing with grace and balance.

From the Heart

There is, however, another scenario that you can make happen. Occasionally, the rider becomes aware of the distracting influence of Self 1 and shuts down its influence of trying to remember things and responds from the heart. What occurs at this point is what good riders do instinctively. They learn the basics, but once those are learned, they listen to their performing self. No time to conjure up what the coach or riding instructor said—events are moving too fast for that. Now they must rely on instincts and feelings that, if they are truly successful riders, have long been absorbed into their performing self. Now their performing self is directing their actions and is in command of the show. This is how good riders are able to exceed even their own best performance. On the other hand, disregarding Self 1 leaves us feeling terribly alone and vulnerable to criticism and the fear of failure. Therefore, casting aside Self 1 is not an easy choice.

The Fear of Failure

What fear of failure does to our concentration is a most interesting phenomenon. Fear of failure is why some athletes undergo something only short of hypnosis before critical engagements to ensure that negative thoughts or doubts about their powers do not creep in before the big performance. To allow that would be to break their concentration and create the self-fulfilling prophecy that was feared in the first place. Although professional athletes have long ago discovered the disabling effects of negative inner thoughts, beginning riders rarely think about such things. When failure occurs they attribute it to their ineptness, not to their lack of concentration caused by the fear of failing. This is an important distinction that never becomes fully untangled in the minds of some riders. Did I not perform well because I don't have the skill, or was I, for some reason, unable to show the skill that I do have? Oddly enough, most beginning riders will choose the former explanation, never realizing the disabling influence their own fears have played in their performance. This negative self-talk tends to grow louder and louder until the rider banishes any risk-taking behavior from his or her repertoire. The rider becomes overly organized, resists anything new, always goes by the book and becomes rigid in his or her riding. This is not a picture from which growth and improvement occur, yet, some riders in every class of competition fall into this trap.

Self-Judgment

What we see is the devastating effect of a hidden self-evaluative character that can be every bit as cruel as the judges scorecard. The net effect may be even more damaging, as we tend to listen to ourselves more often than to an outside observer. The result is that we are unwilling to become vulnerable by risking anything new, and this precludes any form of personal improvement.

How does one separate judgment from feedback? The answer may be surprising. We usually seek out and even sometimes supply ourselves with positive thoughts, but the answer does not lie where you might expect—by heaping positive thoughts upon our naturally occurring negative ones. This is a mistake sometimes made by those closest to us, who may provide little more than a motivational moment. What some have found is that hyped-up motivation unconnected with personal behavior does not last. Worst of all, it often has the effect of implanting more self-doubt than before by providing a picture of a model rider who doesn't exist. What some have not realized is that positive images of oneself can just as easily lead to a negative image, since the exact opposite is easily discernible from contrast with the positive case. In other words, where there is positive there must be negative, the outline of which is amply clear to any rider.

Non-Judgmental Observation

Non-judgmental observation avoids both positive and negative judgments and instead involves only the observed facts. The body takes care of the rest, as the techniques of the best instructors will testify. Their role is to teach the rider to be a good observer of his or her own riding—to acquire a keen eye so that the rider is always aware where critical parts of the body are at what times. The instructor does not shout, "No, that's wrong, get that rein up!" but rather says, "Look where your reins are. Notice the difference." In the first instance the rider may not know how to solve the problem, since she will be wondering where the instructor wants her to place the reins. In the second, the coach is asking the rider first to become aware of her own behavior and then to think about where the reins should be. Where it should be might be where the instructor told her, she remembered from a textbook illustration, or where it was when she last did it right. It is, in short, learning where things feel natural. Notice that nothing positive or negative was said. Instead, the rider was led to become an acute observer of those aspects of the environment most relevant to the performance required and follow his or her natural instincts. In riding, as well as in training and coaching, non-judgmental observation is indispensable for the unbroken concentration you will need for your best performance.

What we have been saying is that external observers may place judgments on our actions, but we must learn not to do so and instead to see our actions as they are, with nothing added. We are always looking for approval of one kind or another and, so, spend more time judging our own behavior than observing what that behavior would actually look like if we could see ourselves in a mirror. In other words, most of us are lousy observers—or feelers—of our own behavior, since our minds are usually filled with distracting self-doubts at the very moment an action is being performed. Breaking this mental habit and observing your own riding non-judgmentally—as a detached umpire or accomplished coach—should be the goal of every rider.

Using Your Performing Self

Now you are ready to begin learning about some of the basics of training and riding. While the concepts, skills and techniques you will learn from the entries that follow will help build strong riding skills, keep in mind that what must follow is your attention to and non judgmental observation of your own riding to create the dynamic and flexible riding personality with which you will exceed your best performance.

Concepts and Skills from A to Z

Introduction

For the beginning rider it will be helpful to read the following entries in the order indicated below before starting with entries A to Z. This will familiarize you with 10 basic concepts essential for good horsemanship and that provide a transition to studying all of the remaining entries.

1. Collection 25
2. Diagonal Aids 26
3. Extension 31
4. Forehands 36
5. Half-halt 40
6. Haunches 42
7. Inside versus Outside 47
8. Lateral Aids 47
9. Rein Aids 56
10. The Vertical 82

Above and Behind the Bit

[**Figure 1**] A horse is "above the bit" when its head is set high and pushing out in front creating a pulling action on the reins. In this case the horse is too extended without a bow at the crest of the neck. A horse is said to be "behind the bit" when his head is set low and behind the *vertical** with head moving down and back from the bit, not into it.

Both above and behind the bit are to be avoided, since the former leads to too much *extension* and possible loss of control of the horse that is pulling on the reins, while the latter leads to too much *collection* in which the horse loses contact with the bit, and in extreme cases, may drop the bit. A horse that is above or below the bit may be corrected by administering a sharp momentary upward action with one, not both, reins. This helps reposition the bit and set the head to a more ideal position at or slightly in front of the vertical.

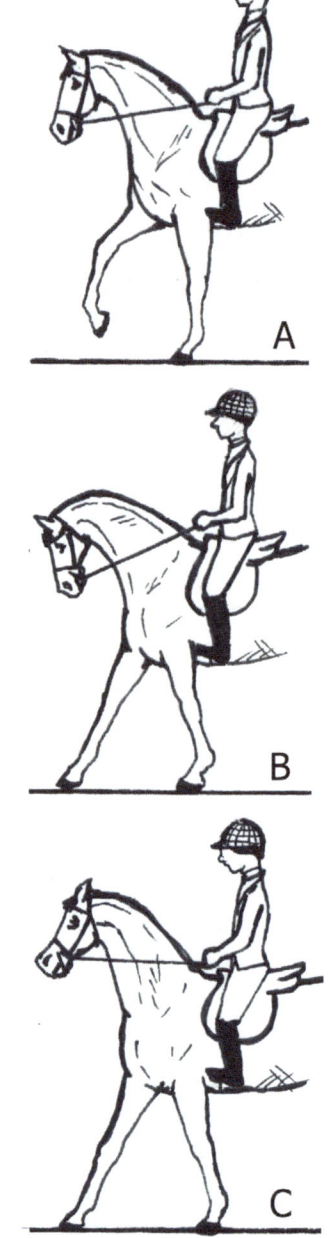

Figure 1. Above and Behind the Bit
(A) Correct contact
(B) Behind the bit
(C) Above the bit

Horse resisting and above the bit.

Backing

See *Rein-back*

---

* Italicized words indicate concepts that appear as separate entries.

Bending, in circle and serpentine

Balance
A horse is balanced when it carries an even proportion of its weight on its *forehand*s and *hindquarters*. Most young horses, however, place more weight on the forehands than hindquarters. The object of training is to transfer this weight from the shoulders to the quarters, usually obtained by *collection*, which raises the forehands and lowers the quarters. When the horse becomes collected, its hind legs step under its body so that the rider feels a slight loosing of tension on the reins. This is called "the horse steps into the bit." By using *leg aids* to apply pressure just behind the girth and pulling back slightly with the reins, the rider is able to make the horse step more under the body with his hind legs and, by restraining him with the reins, cause him to round his back and raise his neck so that his crest comes nearer to the rider. This is the mark of collection.

Bearing (neck) Rein
A bearing or neck rein directs the horse to the left or right by placing one rein against and over the neck of the horse placing tension on the side opposite the direction of the intended movement. The rein pushing on the neck creates the signal for the horse to turn away from the pressure and in the opposite direction. A bearing or neck rein is more predominately used in Western than in English riding. See *Turning on the Haunches* for one of its few applications in English riding.

Behind the Bit
See *Above and Behind the Bit*

Bending, in circle and serpentine
[**Figure 2**] When traveling in a circle, the horse is bent left or right with *lateral* (or same side) *aids*. An inside *indirect rein*, held above and in front of the withers, and an inside leg just behind the girth keeps the horse bent to the inside while a slight tension on the *outside* rein holds the horse's pace. The outside leg, a hand behind the girth, guards against the horse going outside the circle. By action

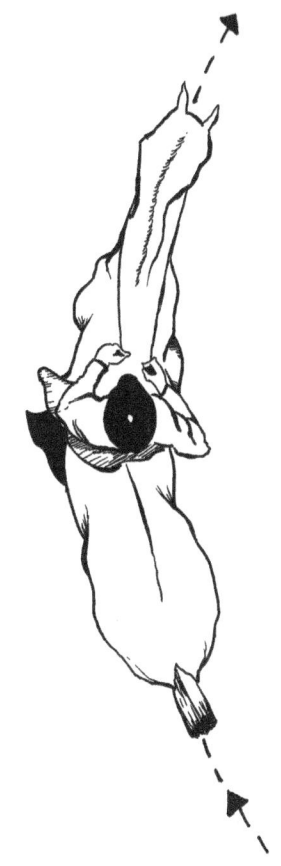

Figure 2. Bending, in a circle and serpentine
Bending in a circle with horse shaped like a half-moon or bow

Bending, in a corner

of the rider's inside leg pushing into the horse just behind the girth, the horse's body bends around this leg while the outside leg, a hand behind the girth, holds the *haunches-in*, creating a horse shaped like a half-moon or bow. When the horse cuts in or out of the circle, use a *leading (open) rein* to direct the horse out or in. These same aids are used in bending the horse in a *serpentine* pattern being careful to cross perpendicular to the centerline.

» *Quick Cue Note:* Bending in a circle. Inside indirect rein, inside leg pushing just behind the girth, outside holding leg a hand behind the girth.

Bending, in a corner

[**Figure 3**] Bending refers to the degree to which a horse is supple in turning from side to side. In turning a corner in a rectangular arena, the horse is bent to the left or right with *diagonal* (opposite side) *aids*. When approaching the corner the rider may first apply an outside *leading rein* to inhibit the horse from cutting the corner. Then, to bend the horse left, use an outside *indirect rein* and inside leg a hand behind the girth pushing the horse into the corner. Together these aids create a bending action while preventing the horse from evading or cutting the corner. Since an indirect rein on the outside is being used to position the horse's head and neck slightly to the inside, care should be taken not to cross the rein over to the other side of the neck. If this is the case apply more inside leg pressure to supplement the rein.

» *Quick Cue Note:* Bending in corner. Outside indirect rein, inside leg pushing a hand behind the girth.

Bitting

[**Figure 4**] Although there are many types of bits, among the most frequently used are the Snaffle, Pelham, Kimberwicke, and Weymouth. The Snaffle is normally used at the beginning of training because it offers the best means of obtaining a steady contact with the horse. Its main advantage at the early stages of training is that

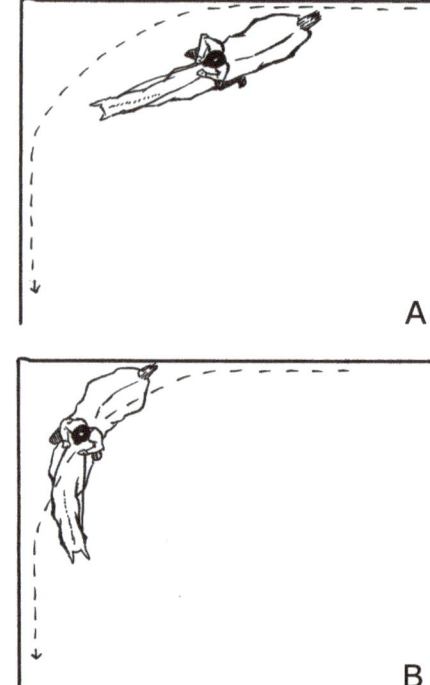

Figure 3. Bending, in a corner
(A) Falling out and (B) falling in a corner

Bending in the corner at the canter.

a snaffle, by working on the tongue and not the roof of the mouth, keeps the head up and therefore shifts some of the horse's weight to the rear, creating better balance. By contrast, a curbed bit, which works on the roof of the mouth, together with a *curb chain* tends to pull the head down. After the horse is trained on a snaffle, a curbed bit, called a Weymouth and a small snaffle, called a *bradoon*, working together as two bits with two separate pairs of reins, provides the best combination of effects. The bradoon picks the head up so that when the curb bit is applied the head is pulled in and the horse's neck becomes bowed with the head at or near the *vertical*. The horse is then said to be collected with forelegs and hindquarters tucked under the body and neck flexed in an arch. (See also *Double Bridle*)

Two additional bits commonly used are the Pelham, which unlike the snaffle has short shanks providing more control, and the Kimberwicke, with still shorter "shanks" in the form of a D ring. The Pelham comes with a straight or jointed (broken) bar and a Kimberwicke with a straight, jointed or curbed bar. Both bits, as well as the Weymouth, can accommodate a curb chain, while a curb chain is not used with a snaffle bit. A distinct feature of the Pelham is that, like the combination Weymouth and bradoon (*double bridle*),

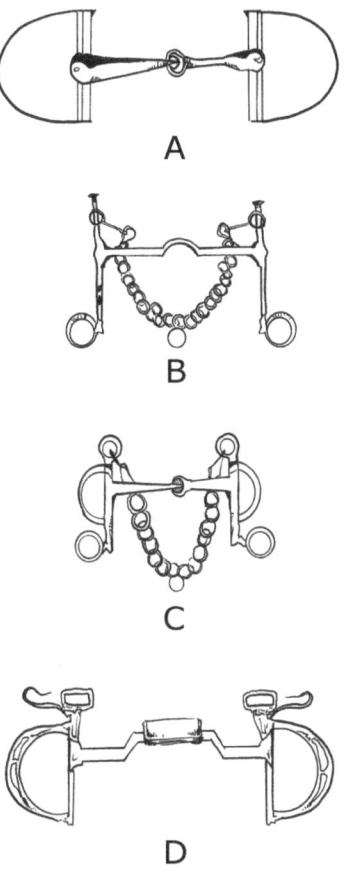

Figure 4. Bitting
(A) Snaffle
(B) Weymouth
(C) Pelham
(D) Kimberwicke

Snaffle bridle.

Bolting

it can accommodate a double set of reins, although with less effect than the combination Weymouth and bradoon to which each is attached a separate set of reins.

Bolting

Bolting is when the horse spontaneously runs away with the rider usually from being frightened. Immediately pulling back on both reins is less effective than turning the horse into a tight circle with a *leading rein* to slow its pace, after which the reins are pulled back and released in short momentary actions (called *half halt*) rather than with a constant pull until the horse comes to a stop. (See also *Shying*)

Bradoon

[**Figure 5**] A bradoon is a small thin snaffle bit used in conjunction with a curbed bit, called a Weymouth, that promotes collection by forcing the head toward the vertical and maintaining a bow just below the crest of the neck. This *"double bridle"* consists of two separate pairs of reins of slightly unequal width to control the effect of each bit, with the smaller width reins attached to the bradoon.

Bucking

[**Figure 6**] The tendency for a horse to buck is most prevalent after being mounted the first time and ridden during initial training. Bucking can be stopped or its effect diminished by moving the horse's head up with both reins held just in front of the withers and simultaneously moving the horse forward. A horse cannot buck if its head is up and moving forward which prevents the horse from making the leap required for a successful buck. During the bucking action the rider should lean back away from the downward pull of the horse's head so as to be higher and behind the motion of the horse and better able to drive the horse forward.

By working with a horse on the ground prior to a first mounting, a horse's tendency to buck can be greatly reduced and sometimes eliminated. This is often accomplished by *lunging* the horse for

Figure 5. Bradoon

Figure 6. Bucking

Turning to correct a buck

several weeks or months before mounting during which time the trainer (1) desensitizes the horse by gradually increasing the intensity of shaking a towel or paper feed bag around and over the horse while another, standing to the side, holds the horse still, then (2) taking a saddle blanket on and off repeatedly, and eventually (3) placing one foot in the stirrup gradually increasing the weight until the rider can stand up on one stirrup without the horse moving.

Cadence

A horse's cadence refers to the elevated (up and down) steps that a horse maintains at the same *rhythm* while moving forward. The effects of cadence can be seen in a high rising (elevated) trot in which more of the horse's energy is spent in creating elevation than in moving forward. A special application of cadence can be seen in a dressage movement, called a *Piaffe*, which is a lively elevated trot in which the horse remains on the spot in a steady cadence as all four feet leave the ground in a split moment of suspension. (See also *Piaffe*)

Canter Depart, methods for

There are several established methods for teaching a horse to canter on the proper lead. Although only one method should eventually be chosen, the rider should be familiar with the different rein and leg aids that are used by different methods in order to arrive at a method best suited for a particular horse and experience of the rider. Before any method is chosen, the horse should be taught the cue to canter in an open field on whatever lead it chooses. Being on the correct lead is important when riding in a circular direction, such as that required by an arena, and differs depending on whether the rider is moving in a clockwise or counter clockwise direction.

Training for the canter depart on the correct lead begins by placing the horse in a position that prevents or makes it difficult for the horse to begin cantering on the wrong lead. Because most horses tend to lead into the canter with their left front leg, the teaching

Canter Depart, methods for

Canter depart illustrating right hind to left foreleg impulsion at the depart.

of leads should begin in the counter clockwise direction requiring the left lead. Most horses favor the left lead because their right rear leg is often the strongest, providing the back right leg to front left leg diagonal impulsion to strike off more easily with their left front leg first.

Most trainers use one of three ways to execute the canter depart in order of difficulty. These also vary in the straightness in which the horse departs in the canter, this being of more concern to the dressage and experienced show rider. Starting from a *trot* in a circular pattern the three methods are:

(a) Pull the rein opposite the desired lead to the outside (toward the rail) so the horse's head moves away from the desired lead. This helps reposition the horse's weight to the outside and "bottles up" or cramps the outside front leg, making it difficult for the horse to throw that leg upward and forward required to lead with that leg. Next, cue with the outside leg just behind the girth. This will encourage the *haunches* to move inward providing the suppleness and flexibility for the inside front leg to move upward and forward. The disadvantage of this approach is that the horse will go into the canter diagonally with head toward the outside (rail) and with haunches-in (toward the center). As the horse becomes accustomed to being cued for the canter, this tendency diminishes. This method can be used with the method below to slowly transition the horse to a straighter canter depart.

» *Quick Cue Note:* Canter depart: method (a). Outside *leading rein* and outside leg just behind the girth to cue the horse.

(b) To execute the canter depart keeping the horse straighter, the rider can use an *indirect* inside *rein* to move the horse's head slightly up and to the outside until the horse's outside eye is just barely visible. Then, cue with the outside leg just behind the girth. The horse should move into the canter straighter, with less *haunches-in*, than with method (a). But, because the head movement is more subtle and haunches straighter, this approach will take more practice.

» *Quick Cue Note:* Canter depart method (b). Inside indirect rein to move the head to the outside, outside leg just behind the girth to cue.

(c) A third approach to the canter depart is executed with both reins and both legs to encourage the horse to go into the canter straight. The rider uses an indirect inside rein to shift the horse's weight to the outside and a *holding* outside *rein* to prevent the horse's head from moving to the outside. The outside leg moves a hand behind the girth but remains passive, providing a holding action preventing the haunches from moving to the outside. The inside leg behind the girth cues the horse. The active inside leg prevents the haunches from moving in, while the outside holding leg prevents the haunches from moving out, keeping the horse straighter.

Canter Depart, problems and remedies

> *Quick Cue Note:* Canter depart method (c). Inside indirect rein to shift the horse's weight to the outside, outside holding rein and holding leg a hand behind the girth, inside leg to cue the horse.

Approach (a) or (b) will be sufficient for most beginning riders and with practice the canter depart will become straighter with either. However, the chance of obtaining the correct lead into the canter will be improved if before cueing for the canter the rider:

> Begins the canter from a trot to provide the horse some initial momentum for throwing the inside foreleg up and forward, and leans slightly back in the saddle and to the side opposite the desired lead to help shift the horse's weight to the outside, making the inside foreleg lighter and easier to strike upward and forward.

To maintain balance, always determine if the horse is on the correct lead by looking down at the horse's shoulder with your eyes without moving your head. After the horse consistently departs on the correct lead in a circle, the rider can begin training for the canter depart from a halt.

Canter Depart, problems and remedies

1. Some horses may try to push their head toward ("lean on") the inside rein when the rider is trying to move the head to the outside for the canter depart with methods (a) and (b) above. For example, if the horse has trouble turning its head to the outside going clockwise, the horse may have a stiff right side preventing the neck from moving easily toward the outside. The rider can execute a half-halt by momentarily pulling only the inside rein once or twice upward above the withers and slightly to the outside to encourage the horse to move its head and weight to that side, freeing up the horse's inside leg for the canter depart. Or, the rider can use a combination of an inside bearing (neck) rein and outside leading rein to move the head to the outside. While either of these methods will assist the

canter depart, the horse should be trained to become equally supple on both sides by practicing the following to prepare for the canter depart:

Haunches-in at walk. In the clockwise direction, the rider can begin preparing for the canter depart on the correct lead by moving the haunches toward the inside with pressure from the left leg a hand behind the girth. A right indirect rein along with a right holding leg at the girth as a pivot point around which the horse is bent helps keep the horse's head in the direction of movement. The horse will be traveling with head forward, right shoulder in front of the left, and haunches toward the inside. In the counter clockwise direction a haunches-in is engaged in the opposite manner by moving the haunches toward the inside with pressure from the right leg a hand behind the girth, a left indirect rein to keep the horse's head forward and a left holding leg to help bend the horse in a slight arc. The horse will be traveling with head forward, right shoulder behind the left and haunches toward the inside. (See also Haunches-in/out)

Half-pass at walk. The canter depart also can be made easier from a half-pass at a walk. While moving forward in the clockwise direction, the rider uses an up and down from ankle to calf to knee outside leg movement to encourage the horse to move into the inside while an inside indirect rein holds the head straight or slightly toward the outside. The right (inside) leg drives the horse forward while moving slightly to the inside. The horse should be moving forward and to the inside on two tracks, with forelegs slightly to the right (inside) of the track on which the hind legs are moving. In either direction the horse should be moving on two tracks, with forelegs slightly inside or outside of the track on which the hind legs are moving. (See also Side Pass, half and true)

Canter Depart, problems and remedies

Both of these movements should be first practiced at a walk and later at a trot and engaged just prior to cueing for the canter to assist a correct canter depart. Half-passing to the inside (in the direction of movement) will make it easier for the horse to pick up the correct lead.

2. When cueing for the canter from a trot, maintain a constant speed. If the horse begins to speed up from your need to continuously cue for the canter, stop the horse and start again. An increase in speed at the trot before the canter provides the horse the opportunity to build the momentum to shift weight to the inside and acquire the wrong lead or change lead in mid-air even when given the appropriate cues.

3. Just as most horses favor, to varying degrees, the left (counter clockwise) lead, some are more flexible and supple than others in moving their necks to one side or the other. Some approaches to teaching the canter depart require the horse to move its head to the left and to the right with equal agility. For example, methods (a) and (b) described under canter depart require that the horse's head be moved with either a leading or indirect rein toward the outside when moving in a circular tract. Most horses will learn to depart on the left lead moving counter clockwise more easily than the reverse, since their right rear leg is often the strongest providing greater back right leg to front left leg diagonal impulsion to strike off with their left front leg first. However, moving in the opposite (clockwise) direction, some horses will have more difficulty in acquiring the correct (right) lead, because the horse's neck must turn toward the left, requiring the horse's right side to be loose and supple enough to make the bend. Some horses will resist the bend to the outside in the clockwise direction, preferring instead to maintain a bend of the neck to the inside, initially making it difficult for the horse to acquire the correct lead in this direction. In such a case, use an indirect right rein to turn the head slightly to the outside together with an up and down

movement of the left leg from ankle to calf to knee to move the horse into a half-pass to the inside before cueing from the outside.

Canter, extended and collected

In an extended canter the head and neck of the horse are allowed to stretch forward and downward placing more weight on the forelegs. This restricts the moment of suspension above the ground so that the horse is not as high as it would be in the collected canter. Little or no neck flexion is visible and there is only slight contact with the bit.

At a collected canter, the horse's head and neck are carried higher with flexion of the neck and greater impulsion than in an extended

The collected canter showing greater flexion of the neck and suspension above ground than an extended canter. (Photo credit: Flickr/Aunt Christina)

canter. The horse's legs are tucked more under the body, shortening the horse's length of stride providing greater elasticity upward for achieving a longer moment of suspension above the ground.

Canter, slowing

To slow the pace at canter or trot, gently close only your hands and fingers to avoid pulling back to take up slack in the reins. This can be combined with a few momentary upward pulls and relaxations of the reins, called a *half-halt*, to slow the horse for a downward transition. Also, use pressure from the legs in addition to closing your hands and fingers in order to drive the hocks under the body, displacing upward some of the horse's forward momentum. This *squeezing up* motion will keep the horse collected into the downward transition and encourage the horse to stand squarely at a halt, with front and back legs aligned with one another.

Capriole

A capriole is an advanced dressage movement performed for exhibition in which the horse jumps off the ground and kicks out with its hind legs at the moment his body is horizontal to the ground.

Capriole: A rarely seen advanced dressage movement performed for exhibition in which the horse jumps off the ground while kicking out with its hind legs. (Photo credit: Flickr/Tx-Gal)

Cavesson

[**Figure 7**] Historically, a cavesson was a band made of padded metal, wood or stiffened material that was placed over the tender cartilage above the horse's nose to provide an active restraint during breeding or training. Today the cavesson is a leather ornamental nose band attached to the bridle that provides no restraint. Far less harsh than its historical predecessor, a "lunging cavesson" is a training device with rings on top and sides for attaching a *lunge line* and *side reins* that replaces the traditional halter for exercising and training. When used in conjunction with a *surcingle* in place of the saddle, the lunging cavesson provides more control for teaching the horse to bend in either direction than if the lunge line were simply connected to a ring at the bottom of a halter. (See also *Lunging*)

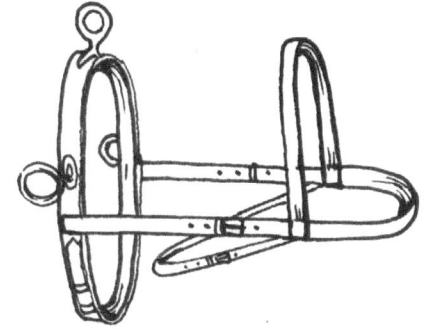

Figure 7. Cavesson

Lunging cavesson illustrating rings for side reins and lunge line

Centerline

The centerline is an imaginary line that bisects lengthwise the center of the arena or practice area. In dressage, the centerline is used as the point at which the rider changes leads or diagonals or begins a change in direction. (See also *Dressage Arena*)

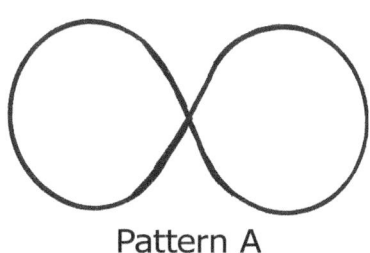

Pattern A

Change of Diagonals (Reins)

[**Figure 8**] A change of diagonals is made at the posting trot to better balance the horse when reversing directions in a circle, crossing the *centerline* in a *serpentine* or at the center of a figure eight pattern. A figure eight pattern is used to practice changing diagonals. This pattern is composed of two adjoining circles of equal size, connected by a short straight line. This connecting line is where the horse straightens its body for a few steps in order to gradually change its bend from one direction to the other. When performing the figure eight pattern correctly the rider straightens her horse for a few steps on the centerline before changing the direction of travel.

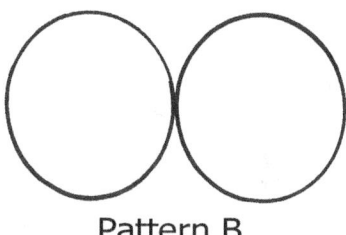

Pattern B

Figure 8. Change of Diagonals (Reins)

(A) Incorrect pattern
(B) Correct pattern

Posting clockwise from the connecting line the rider should be up in the saddle when the horse's left (outside) front leg is in the air. When posting counter clockwise off the connecting line the rider should be up in the saddle when the horse's right (outside) front

Change of Lead, simple

leg is up. When the horse's right front leg is in the air, the horse's left front and right hind leg will be on the ground. When on the wrong diagonal, the rider should sit for two strides and bounce up immediately after the second to return to the opposite (correct) diagonal. The rider's diagonals will change between the circles above and below the centerline. For example, the circle above the connecting line will constitute one diagonal (e.g. the counter clockwise diagonal) and the circle below the centerline the other diagonal (e.g. the clockwise diagonal). The rider can begin practicing changes of diagonals by performing a downward transition from a *posting* to a *sitting trot* at the connecting line and returning to a posting position on the opposite diagonal at the next half of the figure eight. (See *Inside versus Outside*)

» ***Quick Cue Note:*** Change of diagonals. Clockwise, outside (left) front leg up, seat up. Counterclockwise, outside (right) front leg up, seat up.

Change of Lead, simple

[**Figure 9**] Training a horse to change leads at a canter begins in a figure eight pattern composed of two adjoining circles of equal size, connected by a short straight line. A change of lead begins at this centerline, after a downward transition to a walk or trot from a canter. However, starting the new lead from a walk is of greater difficulty. Cues for the canter are reversed at the centerline, so that one lead is engaged for the top half of the figure eight (for example, right lead in the clockwise direction) and the other lead engaged at the return to the centerline for the bottom half (counter clockwise direction) of the figure eight. The horse picks up the new lead as the rider is over the centerline. All walking or trotting steps should occur before the horse reaches the centerline, so the rider must anticipate how many steps her horse will need between leads and perform a downward transition the necessary distance from this centerline. During the lead

Figure 9. Change of Lead, simple

Executing a simple change of lead

change, a horse should take only a few trotting or walking steps. The ideal is two steps (in either gait) during the change, which is the quickest change of lead possible. If the horse needs more steps to balance in order to change leads smoothly, the rider can take up to six steps between leads. The steps need to be in multiples of two, however, for the horse to have the proper sequence to pick up the new lead.

After the horse consistently performs simple changes of leads from a trot, the rider can begin training for changes of leads from a walk and eventually *flying changes of leads* in which the rider goes directly from one lead to the other without transitioning into a walk or trot.

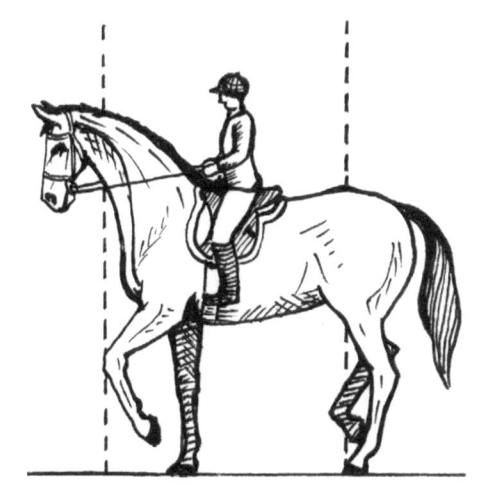

Figure 10. Collection
A collected horse with hocks under the body and neck raised and flexed

Change of Reins
See *Change of Diagonals*

Chin (Lip) Strap
An optional short leather strap attached at the center of the *curb chain* and to each side of the bit to prevent the curb chain from moving forward and over the horse's lip.

Collection
[**Figure 10**] Collection is the degree to which the horse's neck is arched and hocks are under the body. At halt collection is produced by squeezing the horse with both legs into the bit, pushing the horse slightly forward, while restraining any forward movement with the reins. This drives the hind legs and forelegs under the body, "collecting" energy between them, readying the horse for the "spring" needed for an upward transition, for example, from a halt to a canter.

Figure 11. Counter Canter
The counter canter showing the outside leg leading

Counter Canter
[**Figure 11**] The counter canter requires the horse to take the wrong lead when traveling in a circle. The horse will then be on the outside rather than the inside lead it normally uses to maintain balance when traveling in a circular pattern. In tests of dressage, its

purpose is to determine if the rider has control of the horse's leads independent of direction.

Croup (Topline)

[**Figure 12**] The croup of a horse is the top of the horse extending from the rump to the tail. The croup should flow smoothly into the tail and continue forward to the withers in a level line, providing a sense of flow and continuity across the full length of the horse's back, called the top line.

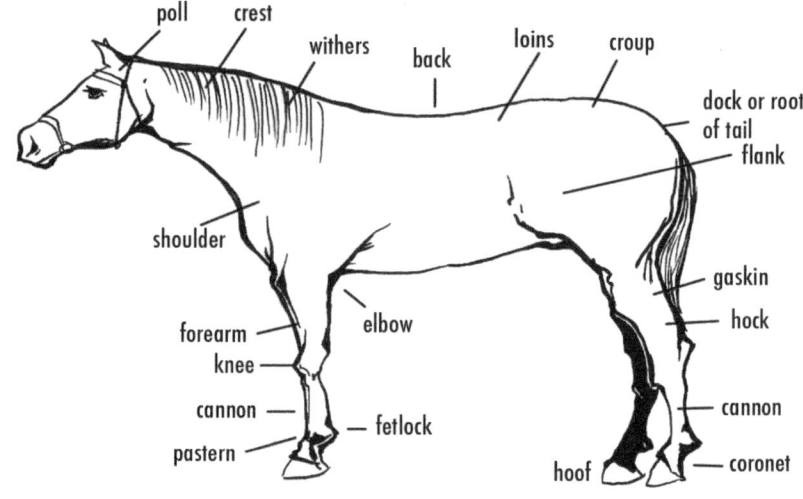

Figure 12. Croup (Topline)
Proper croup and topline and other parts of the horse

Curb Chain

[**Figure 13**] A small chain or leather strap running under the horse's chin and affixed to each side of the bit to provide pressure under the chin and a leverage point for pushing the curb or bar of the bit onto the roof of the horse's mouth when the shanks are activated by the reins. A curb chain may be used in conjunction with a *lip strap* that prevents the curb chain from moving forward and over the lip of the horse.

Diagonal Aids

Diagonal aids are leg and rein aids applied from opposite sides of the horse, as in the simultaneous use of a left *indirect rein* and right leg aid to execute a *canter depart (method b)* on the left lead. *Lateral aids* refer to leg and rein aids applied from the same side of the horse, as in the simultaneous use of a left indirect rein and left leg aid to execute a left *shoulder in*.

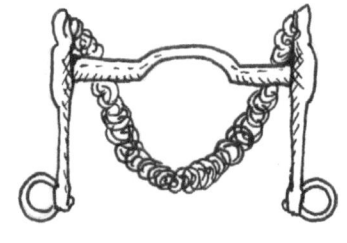

Figure 13. Curb Chain
Curb chain shown on a Weymouth bit

Diagonals

See *Change of Diagonals*

Direct Rein

For a direct rein, the reins are held in a straight line level with the rider's elbow to the horse's mouth, regardless of the position of the horse's head. The direct rein is the means by which collection or a decrease of pace is obtained by affecting the balance of the horse from foreleg to haunch as opposed to from side to side. Another of its uses is to keep the horse's head and neck straight, with no evidence of bending or flexing to either side. Other types of reins include the *indirect rein*, *open or leading rein*, *bearing rein*, and *pulley rein*. (See also *Rein Aids*)

Double Bridle

[**Figure 14**] A "double bridle" is a curbed bit in combination with a small snaffle, called a *bradoon*, thus creating a bridle with two separate bits each with its own set of reins. The bradoon picks the head up so that when the curb bit is applied the head is pulled in and the horse's neck becomes bowed with the head at or near the *vertical*. The horse is then said to be collected with forelegs and hindquarters tucked under the body and neck flexed in an arch. Double bridles are mostly used in performance classes requiring high degrees of collection, such as Dressage, Park and English Pleasure. (See also *Bitting*)

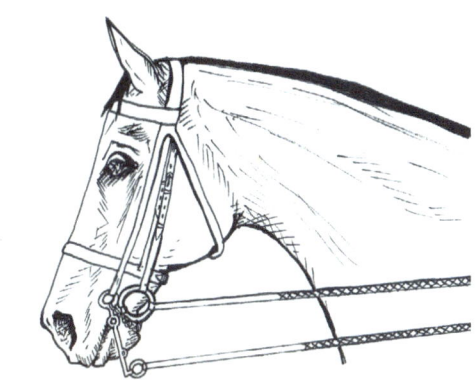

Figure 14. Double Bridle

Double bridle shown with Bradoon and Weymouth bits

Double bridle with a Bradoon bit on top collecting and setting the horse's head and a Weymouth bit beneath controlling forward motion and direction. Excess reins are gathered on the left.

Dressage, arena

[Figure 15] The standard dressage arena consists of a 20 meters (66 feet) by 60 meters (197 feet) rectangle, although a smaller arena (66 by 130 feet) is also used. In either case letters are affixed to the sides of the rectangle to designate precisely where practiced maneuvers are to take place. Although often a point of interest, there is no known historical record as to how the letters where chosen. An imaginary "X" marks the center of the rectangle, where during tests of dressage, each rider entering begins and ends with a salute to Emperor Charles the VI of Austria, who in 1729 built the indoor riding hall in Vienna, Austria, which has been home to the *Spanish Riding School*.

Figure 15. Dressage, arena
Dressage arena with optional RSVP points

Dressage, definition

A general definition of the purpose of dressage, as prepared by the International Equestrian Authority *(FEI)*, includes development of the physique and ability of the horse, leading to a horse that is calm, supple, loose and flexible, and also confident, attentive and keen. These qualities result from:

- lightness of the forehand, and engagement of the hindquarters, originating in a lively impulsion,
- the acceptance of the bridle, with submissiveness, and without any tension or resistance, so that,
- the horse gives the impression of doing of his own accord what is required of him. (See also *FEI, Fédération Equestre Internationale*)

Regardless of one's intended purpose, these are qualities that apply to all levels and types of horsemanship.

Dressage, exercise patterns

Some of the basic exercise patterns for making a horse supple and teaching the basics of dressage include:

- Lateral serpentine (tight or broad, 6 or 3 turns back and forth across the centerline of the arena)
- Vertical serpentine (up and down the length of the arena)
- Figure eight
- Circle (half arena)
- Circle (quarter arena, "volte")

Others include:

Figure eight within the circle: The horse moves in a figure eight pattern within a larger circle and rein and leg aids are changed with each circle at the midpoint.

Change within the circle: The horse moves in two half *volte*'s by creating an S pattern through the middle of a large circle. The S pattern through the middle is reversed at each half circle to change the direction of the horse.

Half volte and change: The horse is directed along the length of the arena, then turns to the middle and returns to the point of origin, creating a tear drop pattern.

Dressage, levels of

The International Equestrian Authority (*FEI*) governs the rules and tests of dressage. In the U.S. the dressage levels are: Introductory, Training Level; First, Second, Third, and Fourth Levels; Prix St. Georges; Intermediate; and Grand Prix. The first five levels (Introductory through Level 3) include the basic requirements for schooling all riding horses, whatever the purpose. The Third Level trains toward activities that require an intensely active and supple horse, e.g. Three-Day Event (endurance, dressage, and jumping) horses. The more advanced levels of dressage are highly specialized and for training horses that are almost exclusively used for exhibition. Although dressage requirements at the various levels of difficulty undergo periodic changes, some of the requirements

Dressage, levels of

for the Introductory through Fourth Levels have included (italics indicate text entries):

Introductory Level—*rising (posting) trot*, free and medium walks, *change of reins* (diagonals).

Training Level—working canter on right and left lead (20 meters), track right and left, *working trot*, allowing horse to stretch forward and downward.

First Level—*serpentines* at trot, lengthened strides at trot and canter in circles (15 and 20 meters), *change of rein* (diagonal), *leg-yield* right/left.

Second Level—travers (*haunches-in*), renvers (*haunches out*), collected canter, *counter canter, rein-back, turning on the haunches*, simple *change of lead, shoulder in, serpentine* canter without change of lead, shorten stride in walk.

Third Level—*extended canter*, serpentine canter with simple *change of lead, flying change of lead*, immediate depart collected trot.

Fourth Level—*half/quarter pirouette*, three flying change of leads, very *collected canter*.

Some of the requirements at more advanced levels (Prix St. Georges, Intermediate, and Grand Prix) are canter at half-pass with flying change of leads, canter *pirouettes, piaffe* and *passage*, and transitions from passage to piaffe and from piaffe to passage.

Computer animations and illustrations of the most recent movements required for dressage tests are available from: *www.whinnywidgets.com.*

Ears, movement of

The ears are one of the most "telling" parts of the horse, the proper position of which should be erect and forward. Ears laid back indicate the horse's distraction, stiffness or uneasiness, often telegraphing to the attentive rider upcoming disobedience.

Extension

[**Figure 16**] Extension is the length of a horse's stride through impulsion. A trained horse and rider should be able to exhibit *extension* (increased length of stride through impulsion with only minor *flexion*) as well as *collection* (head flexed and hocks well under the horse). Extension is emphasized in Hunter Pleasure and Dressage classes and collection is emphasized in Dressage, English Pleasure and Park classes. However, all equestrian purposes require some proportion of each.

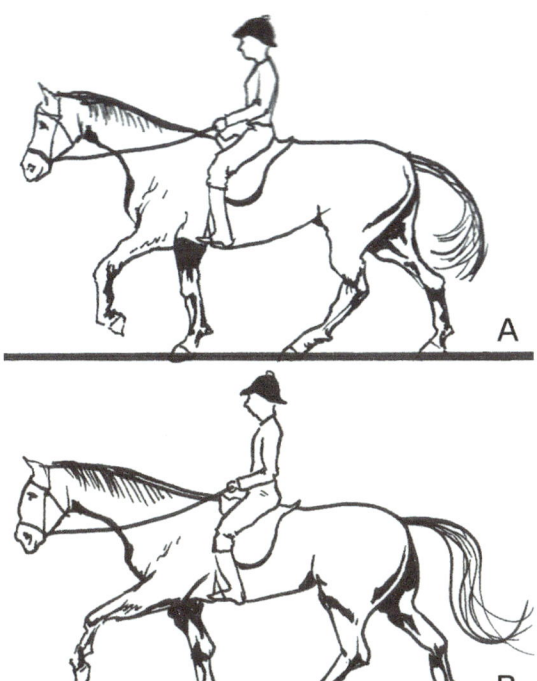

Figure 16. Extension

Moving from (A) a normal walk to (B) an extended walk with greater reach and impulsion

Horse at extended walk with collection and impulsion.

Eyes, rider's

The rider's eyes should follow the movement of the horse and be looking ahead of where the horse is moving.

When checking to see if the horse is on the correct lead, the rider maintains balance by looking down with eyes only without moving the head, leaning forward or hanging over the horse's shoulder.

When losing a stirrup, the rider should be able to insert her foot into the stirrup without dropping her eyes to see where it is. By dropping both feet out of the stirrups, the rider can practice feeling where a stirrup hits in relation to the ankle bone. The bottoms of the stirrups should just reach the rider's ankles.

FEI (Fédération Equestre Internationale)

The FEI is the international governing body of equestrian sport recognized by the International Olympic Committee. It is the organization that establishes rules and regulations for the conduct of international equestrian events in the Jumping, Dressage, Eventing, Driving, Vaulting and Endurance Riding disciplines. This includes the supervision and maintenance of the health and welfare of the horses as well as respect for the principles of horsemanship. The FEI was founded in 1921 when delegates from ten countries met in Lausanne, Switzerland to discuss the formation of an international federation. Presently there are over 130 member countries. The official web sites of the FEI are: *www.fei.org* (Lausanne, Switzerland) and *www.usef.org* (Lexington, Kentucky). FEI rules and publications may be obtained from: Fédération Equestre Internationale, Avenue Mon Repos 24, PO Box 157, 1000 Lausanne 5, Switzerland.

Flexion

Flexion is the amount the horse's head moves toward the *vertical* driven by the haunches, not by pulling the reins. It is executed with both legs squeezing just behind the girth at the same time slight pressure is applied on the bit. The rider's hands alternating laterally back and forth, called a vibrating hand, can encourage yield and flexion in the horse's mouth if the horse at first hesitates. Raising both reins, called a *lifting hand,* can correct a horse that is over-

Flying Change of Lead

Horse's head bowed and moving toward the vertical illustrating flexion achieved by squeezing both legs just behind the girth at the same time slight pressure is applied to the bit.

flexed or boring down on the bit and correct a heavy forehand in which the horse's head hangs too low. (See also *Collection*)

Flying Change of Lead

[**Figure 17**] After the horse consistently changes leads by way of a downward transition to a walk or trot at the connecting line of a figure eight pattern, the rider can begin training for flying changes of leads. For a flying change of lead, the rider asks the horse to switch leads at the completion of the first circle of a figure eight without breaking into either a walk or a trot, as would be the case for a simple change of leads.

To begin the flying change of lead, the rider circles in the clockwise direction. On approaching the end of the circle at the connecting line, where the two halves of the figure eight pattern meet, the rider begins to even out the pressure from her hand and leg positions to straighten the horse and uses a series of *half-halts* consisting of a few momentary pulls and relaxations of the reins to alert and "set up" the horse for the change. The rider keeps the horse from

Figure 17. Flying Change of Lead

A flying change of lead from right to left

Flying Change of Lead

Flying change of lead in which both front legs are in the air. Horse is pushing off left hind leg and changing to the right lead. (Photo credit: Flickr/nikki_tate)

leaning toward the upcoming counterclockwise direction of travel by using a *holding* left leg and left *neck rein*. Then, using a left indirect rein and drawing the right leg back a hand behind the girth, the rider cues the horse as it reaches the center point of the figure eight. By, at first, keeping the horse from learning in the upcoming direction of travel, the rider prevents placing weight on the inside foreleg which would make the change to the correct lead more difficult. Training for the *half-pass*, in which a slight up and down motion from ankle to calf to knee is used to move the horse to one side and lightening him on the other, is excellent training in preparation for a flying change of leads.

To do a flying change, the horse must be well balanced and not moving toward the outside of the first circle, since this would place excess weight onto the side of the horse which must be light for the change. As the lead is being changed the horse should not "fall" into the new direction, but should lift its front end slightly and switch in one quick motion of the front leg, landing on the new lead all at once. Just after the change, the rider should bend her horse in the new direction of travel, so the horse will be balanced around the circle.

Flying Change of Lead, problems and remedies

1. If the horse refuses to perform flying changes of leads at the canter in a figure eight pattern, gradually tighten the pattern until the correct lead is obtained. If the horse still has difficulty, practice flying changes leads in a straight line by cantering 30 feet on one lead and then giving the signal to change and cantering on the new lead for the next 30 feet. The back and forth change of leads should be done three or four times before stopping and repeated as often as necessary until the correct change of leads is obtain.

2. Flying change of leads can also be practiced by weaving in and out through a set of stakes placed into the ground 16 feet apart. The stakes should not be greater than 16 feet apart to force the horse to change leads. The object is to work the horse tightly in and out around each of the stakes increasing the speed as the horse becomes more proficient. To begin, walk and trot the horse through the stakes weaving to the right of one and to the left of the next. After the horse knows what is wanted, work at a collected canter, alternating the leg and rein cues as you move in and out of the stakes. If you are on the right of one stake moving to the left of the next, you would cue with the right leg and lift the left rein lightening the horse on the side of the new lead. When moving back from the inside of the following stake to the outside of the next, you would cue with the left leg and lift the right reign. The change of leads is made broadside to the stakes.

Forehands (Forelegs)

Forehands (Forelegs)

Technically, the forehands refers to that part of the horse that is in front of the rider. But, generally, it refers to the two front legs of the horse. It is used in phrases such as *turning on the forehands*, in which the horse's weight is shifted to his front legs one crossing over the other as it turns.

Gaits

[**Figure 18**] All horses have at least four natural gaits: the walk, trot, canter and hand gallop, and full or racing gallop.

The walk can be divided into a collected walk, in which the horse is in contact with the bit with head arched and forehands and haunches under the body of the horse; a relaxed (medium) walk, in which the rider loosens the reins; and an extended walk, in which the rider extends his reins allowing the horse to stretch his head and neck forward and downward but still maintains some impulsion from behind and some contact on the bit. The walk is a four beat movement starting with the right hind leg, the right front leg, the left hind leg, and finally the left front leg.

The trot can be divided into the working (normal) trot, collected trot, and extended trot (see *Trot*) that are distinguished more by the amount of extension, or length of stride exhibited by the horse, than its speed. Another type of trot is the *sitting trot*, but this is a term that may be applied to the other types of trots as well, such as a working trot with the rider sitting. In a trot the horse moves in a two beat rhythm in which the right hind and left front legs hit the ground together, followed a moment later by the left hind and right front legs together with a brief moment of suspension between in which all four legs are off the ground. The trot is a two-beat diagonal gait in which the left front leg and right hind leg work together as do the right front leg and left hind leg, providing a diagonal means of impulsion. This gait has a period of suspension in which the horse springs from one diagonal to the other leaving a moment in which all four legs are off the ground. Being on the

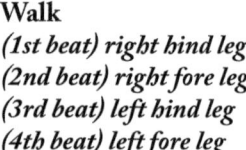

Walk
(1st beat) *right hind leg*
(2nd beat) *right fore leg*
(3rd beat) *left hind leg*
(4th beat) *left fore leg*

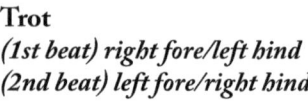

Trot
(1st beat) *right fore/left hind*
(2nd beat) *left fore/right hind*

Canter and Hand Gallop
Right Lead:
(1st beat) *left hind leg*
(2nd beat) *right hind/left fore*
(3rd beat) *right fore leg*

Full Gallop
Right Lead:
(1st beat) *left hind leg*
(2nd beat) *right hind leg*
(3rd beat) *left fore leg*
(4th beat) *right fore leg*

Figure 18. Gaits

Pattern of footfalls for the walk, trot, canter and hand gallop and full gallop

Gaits

Rider posting at a working trot on the inside (clockwise) diagonal in which the rider is up in the saddle when the left foreleg and right hind leg are in the air.

correct *diagonal* at a posting trot when moving in a circular direction is important for maintaining the horse's balance. Since the trot has two beats each stride and a moment in mid-air between them, it is more comfortable for the rider and horse together to rise up and down every other beat, called posting. When trotting, the diagonal on which the rider is on is opposite the diagonal on which the rider is posting when up in the saddle.

The canter can be divided into the canter and hand gallop. In both, the horse's feet move in a three beat rhythm, and therefore are considered a single gait. But a horse in a "hand gallop" will be moving approximately four miles per hour (6.4 km) faster than in a canter, a canter typically being at a rate of about 10–12 mph (16–19 km) and the hand gallop at the rate of about 14–16 mph (23–26 km). This gait also has a brief moment of suspension in which all four legs are off the ground. If the horse is moving in the clockwise direction calling for the right lead, the order of foot falls begins with the left hind leg, then both the right hind leg and left front leg are on the ground at the same time, followed by the right front leg—creating a three beat gait. When moving in the counter clockwise direction calling for the left lead, the order of foot falls

Gaits

Horse collected at trot illustrating the brief moment of suspension of the right foreleg and left hind leg.

is reversed beginning with the right hind leg, then left hind and right front legs simultaneously, and then the left front leg. Using the proper lead when moving in a circular motion helps maintain a horse's balance around the corners.

A full or racing gallop is similar to the canter, but the horse's legs move one at a time, creating a four beat movement, in which all four feet are momentarily off the ground in each stride and strike so near to one another that the four beats blend. When slowed to a hand gallop or still slower, to a canter, the horse's foot falls return to a three beat gait. When moving in the counter clockwise direction calling for the left lead, the order of foot falls begins with the right hind leg, followed by the left hind leg, followed by the right front leg and finally the left front leg. When moving in the clockwise direction calling for the right lead, the order of foot falls is reversed beginning with the left hind leg, followed by the right hind leg, followed by the left front leg, and finally the right front leg. The full or racing four beat gait is not used in the show arena and would be scored as a fault.

While horses with four gaits are the most common, some horses are naturally inclined to have other gaits, the Tennessee walking

Rider at canter in which the horse is moving in a three beat rhythm and all four feet are simultaneously off the ground in a brief moment of suspension.

horse and Peruvian Paso being among these. These "gaited" horses usually have a gait that replaces the trot to provide a smoother ride than would the posting trot but maintaining or surpassing its speed. These gaited horses often came into prominence for specialized purposes and their natural inborn tendencies emphasized in training and breeding. For example, the Tennessee Walker became prominent for its use in inspecting long rows of tobacco in which the rider sought a more comfortable, less rising or choppy, gait than would be provided by posting at the trot.

Gallop, hand and full

See *Gaits*

Half-halt

Half-halt
The "half-halt" is used to collect the horse and get the horse to move into the bit, slowing the cadence and lightening the horse for more complex movements. It is executed with a few momentary upward pulls and relaxations of the reins with a simultaneous squeezing motion with left and right leg aids to promote collection.

A half halt may also be used to alert the horse for an impending command and for corrective "aiding" actions. For example, in a canter depart a unilateral (single-rein) half-halt may be used with the inside rein to help shift the horse's weight to the outside, lightening the inside to promote going into the correct lead. Another example is encouraging a horse into a slower pace that has just learned to canter. Both reins are pulled in short momentary actions, while slight pressure is exerted with both legs. This combination of a half halt and leg aids preserves the horse's collection during a transition, making the horse go through the transition with the hind legs placed well under the body, as would be required for the transition from a hand gallop back to a canter.

Half-pass
See *Side Pass, half and true*

Halts
The true halt should be practiced from the collected trot. The horse should end the movement without taking any steps at the walk (a true halt). The horse should not move slowly into a halt. At the halt the horse should be standing straight, with hind legs well under the body and weight equally balanced on all four legs, fore and hind legs side by side. The horse should not lose contact with the bit. To achieve a true halt, pressure from both legs accompanies a slight squeezing, not pulling, action of the reins to ensure the horse stops square, with forelegs slightly under the horse and even with each other.

Hand Gallop

The "hand gallop" is distinguished from the "full or racing gallop" in that the hand gallop is less extended and is a three-beat gait, while the full gallop, which calls for greater pace and extension, requires each hoof to be placed separately creating four beats. The phrase "hand gallop" denotes that the rider is controlling the degree of the horse's extension with the reins, preventing the horse from extending into a four-beat (full gallop) rhythm. (See also *Gaits*)

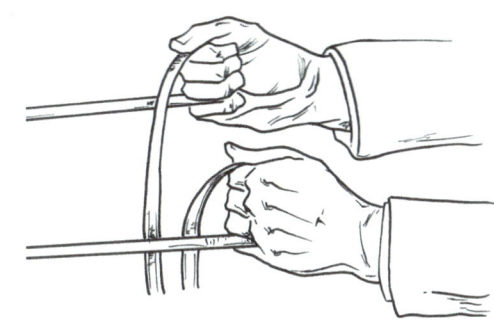

Figure 19. Hands, placement of
Proper grasp of the reins

Hands, placement of

[**Figure 19**] The proper position of the rider's hands should be just over and slightly in front of the withers and in a direct line from the rider's elbow to the horse's mouth. Forearms and wrists should be straight with thumbs about four inches apart. A well-trained horse should respond to a rider by just closing her hands to softly tighten the reins. The action of the reins should not be applied from a loose rein but from a slight squeezing of the hands from reins that are slightly taut.

Rider illustrating proper position of hands with forearms and wrists aligned.

Hand, measure of a horse's height

A "hand" used as a measure of a horse's height is equal to the width of an average hand, or about 4 inches. It was used in early horsemanship to measure the approximate height of a horse at

Haunches (hindquarters)

its withers. For example, the height of a horse at 14 and one-half hands, referred to as 14.2 ("fourteen-two"), would equal approximately 58 inches. But, this method of measurement can be notoriously inaccurate, especially in buying or selling a horse. An accurate measurement of a horse's height can only be recorded with a graduated horse measuring stick that expands vertically with an arm that swings horizontally over the horse's withers at a 90 degree angle while the horse is standing on level ground.

Haunches (hindquarters)

Haunches refer to the posterior of the horse encompassing the hips that may at times include the two back legs—often used synonymously with the word "*hindquarters*." It is used in phrases such as "*turning on the haunches*" in which the horse is taught to pivot with the preponderance of weight on his hind legs, one crossing over the other as he turns. (See also *Croup*)

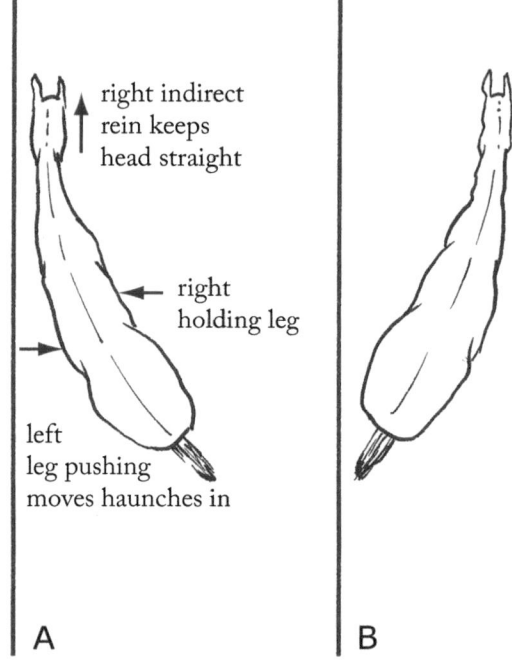

Figure 20. Haunches-in/out

(A) Haunches-in (head to the rail)
(B) Haunches-out (tail to the rail)

Haunches-in/out

[**Figure 20**] Haunches-in is a *half-pass* at a walk or trot on the rail in which the horse's head is parallel to the rail with the front legs on the track, hind legs inside the track and the horse is bent toward the direction of movement (also called *travers*). Haunches-out is opposite to haunches-in, in which the horse's tail is turned into the rail with the front legs in from the track and hind legs on the track (also called *renvers*). Both haunches-in and haunches-out are required for the intermediate and advanced levels of dressage and are important exercises for getting ready for the half and full side pass. (See also *Side Pass, half and true* and *Two Tracking*)

Haunches-in or out is executed with a combination of leg and rein aids. To move the horse into a haunches-in position (Figure 20A, head parallel to rail) in the clockwise direction, use a left (outside) leg a hand behind the girth to push the haunches to the inside of the track and to drive the horse forward. Use a right indirect rein with slight tension to the inside to bend the horse in the direction of movement. A right (inside) holding leg at the girth serves as

Haunches-in/out

Haunches-in illustrating front and hind legs on different tracks.

a pivot point to complement the right indirect rein to maintain a uniform bend. For haunches-out in the clockwise direction (Figure 20B, tail to rail), the cues are reversed: right leg a hand behind the girth pushing and driving the horse forward and left leg holding at the girth and left indirect rein slightly to the outside to maintain the bend and position the head in the direction of movement. Start your haunches-in from a small circle to create the bend and then go straight, returning to the circle if you lose the bend.

» *Quick Cue Note:* Haunches-in clockwise. Left leg a hand behind the girth pushing and driving, right indirect rein to position the head slightly to the inside and right leg at the girth holding to maintain the bend. Haunches-out clockwise. Right leg a hand behind the girth pushing and driving, left indirect rein to position the head slightly to the left and left leg at the girth holding.

Head, lowering or raising of

A unilateral (single rein) *half-halt* can be used to make a horse carry its head and neck lower or higher. In the case of lowering the head and neck, one rein is momentarily pulled downward in the direction of the rider's opposite hip. The opposite rein is kept taught to prevent the horse's head from turning. If a higher position of head and neck is desired, one rein is momentarily pulled higher but this time toward the opposite side of the rider's chest. The rider should not raise or lower the horse's head with both reins or with a constant pull at the reins.

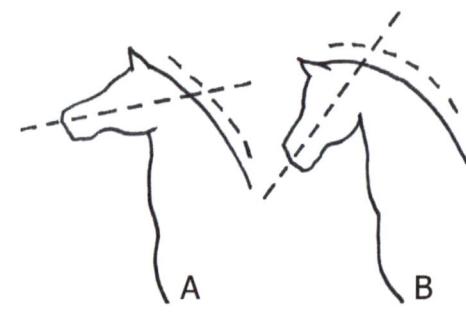

Figure 21. Head, proper position of

(A) Improper headset with neck cocked out
(B) Proper head set with head drawn downward and neck flexed

Head, proper position of

[**Figure 21**] The position of a horse's head from the *vertical* will depend upon the amount of training devoted to collection. A horse with tight neck muscles will need to be made more supple before much collection and a desirable "head set" can be achieved. *Lunging* a young horse with a lunging *cavesson*, *surcingle* and *side reins* is one method of suppling the neck muscles and promoting collection by moving the horse's head closer to the vertical in small degrees. With horses that have been sufficiently schooled, to obtain

Horse with head at the vertical.

a proper head set in the collected paces of a posting trot and canter, the line of the head should be more or less vertical to the ground and neck arched. The horse's head, however, should not be behind the vertical (pointing inward toward the chest), which would inhibit forward movement.

Hocks, cow and bowed

[**Figure 22**] Hocks are a region in the hind legs of the horse corresponding to the ankle but elevated and bending backward. When correctly aligned, a vertical line can be drawn from the center point of the hindquarter down the leg to the center point of the hoof. "Cow hocks" (Figures 22A and 22B) and "Bowed hocks" are two confirmation faults that move the hocks from this vertical line. "Cow hocks," which is the more common, is a fault in which the hind legs are bent inward with hocks pointing outward, away from one another. "Bowed hocks" is a fault, opposite to cow hocks, in which the horse's hind legs are bent outward with hocks pointing inward. Each of these faults can reduce a horse's impulsion and steadiness.

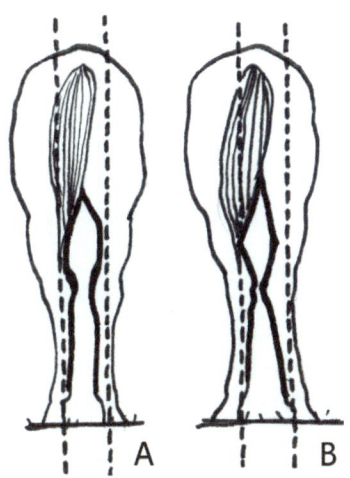

Figure 22. Hocks, cow

(A) Moderate cow hocks with legs slightly inward; (B) Severe cow hocks with hind legs bent inward and hocks pointing outward

Holding (supporting) Leg

A holding (also called supporting) leg is a leg aid used passively, that is, with only slight contact with the horse, in order to prevent the horse from moving in that direction while other aids are being used. For example, in *turning on the haunches* an outside holding leg prevents the horse from moving toward the outside while the horse pivots on its hind legs. In *haunches-in/out* a holding leg is used as a pivot or pressure point combined with an indirect rein to encourage the horse to bend its haunches inward or outward from the track.

Holding (supporting) Rein

A holding (also called supporting) rein is a rein aid used passively, with only slight contact with the bit, in order to prevent the horse from moving forward while other aids are being used. For example, in *turning on the forehand* an outside holding rein is used to prevent

Horse with excellent hocks with legs straight from center of the hindquarter to the center point of the hocks.

45

the horse from moving forward while the opposite rein turns the horse to the inside.

Hunter Equitation, some tests of performance

Among the tests of performance that may be required in Hunter Equitation classes are (italics indicate text entries):

- *Halt* (4 to 6 seconds) and/or back.
- *Hand gallop* and halt.
- *Figure eight at trot* (changing diagonals).
- *Figure eight at canter* on correct lead (simple change of lead).
- Work collectively at walk, *trot*, or *canter*.
- Pull up and halt (4 to 6 seconds).
- Ride without stirrups or drop and pick up stirrups.
- *Dismount* and *mount*.
- *Turn on the forehand at halt*.
- Figure eight at canter on correct lead demonstrating *flying change of lead*.
- Execute a three loop *serpentine* at a trot on correct *diagonals* and/or canter on correct leads demonstrating simple or flying changes of lead.
- Change of leads on a line demonstrating a simple or *flying change of lead*.
- Canter on counter lead (*counter canter*).
- *Turn on the haunches* from the walk.
- Demonstration ride of approximately one minute. (This test allows the rider to demonstrate the level of her skill by making up her own pattern of movements).
- The above tests are exclusive of those that require jumping.

Impulsion

Impulsion is a horse's ability to move forward with elasticity, originating with thrust from the haunches. For example at a walk the horse should have steady impulsion from behind and not plod along.

Indirect Rein

The indirect rein controls movement to the side (lateral) work, such as bending in a circle or turning in which the horse must bend in the same direction that it is moving.

In moving in a circle, an inside indirect rein held above and in front of the withers causes the horse's head and neck to bend toward the inside just enough for the corner of the horse's eye to be visible to the rider. This same rein also displaces the horse's weight from the inside to the outside shoulder, thus affecting the balance from side to side rather than from foreleg to haunch as would be the case with a direct rein.

For example, to bend the horse to the right, a right indirect rein moves above and in front of the withers, as the left hand yields to the same degree that the right indirect rein takes up. The rider now feels slightly more pressure in the right hand than in the left. An indirect rein is usually coordinated with the use of a leg aid just behind the girth on the same side to create a bend from head to haunches that keeps the horse tracking in a curved position. (See also *Rein Aids*)

Inside versus Outside

"Inside" refers to the side nearest the center of the ring and "outside" to the side nearest the rail or outer edge of the ring. For example, when the horse is moving around the ring to the left, that is, in the counter clockwise direction, the horse's left shoulder is on the inside, the side toward which the horse is bending. When cantering in a straight line, the inside is the same side as the lead the horse is on and when trotting it is the opposite *diagonal* to the one that is up.

Lateral Aids

Lateral aids are aids that are executed from the same side of the horse, as when an indirect left rein and left leg aid are used to bend the horse in circling to the left.

Lateral Work

Lateral Work

Lateral work includes all those movements in which the horse not only steps forward but also sideways, as in a *half-pass* or *shoulder in* at walk or trot.

Leading (open) Rein

A leading rein (also called open rein) is used primarily in turning the horse by holding one rein out to the side of the horse's neck in the direction of movement. A leading rein has no application to bending or restraining and is used primarily in turning.

Leads

See *Caner Depart*

Leg Aids

There are three basic placements of the leg in which it acts as an aid: in front of the girth toward the horse's shoulder, just behind the girth, and a hand (about four inches) behind the girth. In front of the girth may imbalance the rider and therefore is only recommended for advanced riders and higher levels of dressage. The back edge of the girth approximates the middle of the horse, where the horse is most affected by the legs. This is where the leg has maximum driving power for forward movement. Accordingly, it is just behind the girth where the inside leg remains most of the time to maintain driving and bending influence.

Whereas a rider's leg just behind the girth affects the horse as a whole, a leg a hand behind the girth controls only lateral displacement of the haunches, a sideways action that does not influence the horse's forward movement. For example, in moving counter clockwise with haunches out (to the rail), the rider's inside leg a hand behind the girth moves the haunches toward the rail by applying slight steady pressure, while the outside holding leg placed just behind the girth creating a pivot point assists in bending the horse in an arc. Each of these leg aids work together to assume their primary function of bending the horse from head to tail.

Leg-yielding

Leg-yielding is a lateral movement in which the horse moves forward and slightly sideways at the same time. While moving forward the horse is made to yield left without turning the horse or a slowing of forward movement by using more pressure with the right rein than the left, turning the horse's head slightly away from the direction to which the horse is yielding, and using a leg aid on the same (right) side just behind the girth to create enough pressure to encourage the horse to yield to the left while moving forward creating a diagonal path. In yielding left, the left rein is kept taught providing a holding action preventing the horse's head and neck from turning to the right. The horse will be moving forward and diagonally at the same time with body straight and head slightly to the right. The simultaneous use of the left and right reins keeps the horse's body straight allowing the continuation of the horse's normal pace while yielding. To yield to the right, the aids are reversed. Leg-yield right and leg-yield left are required in the beginning levels of dressage, as well as on the trail where an obstruction may require movement forward and diagonally at the same time. In yielding to the left or right the horse's fore and hind legs are on the same or nearly the same tracks, contrary to a *half-pass* where the horse is moving forward and to the side at the same time with front and back legs on noticeably different tracts or a side pass where the horse's front and hind legs are moving only to the side with no forward movement. (See also *Two Tracking*)

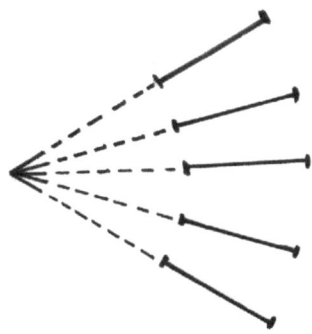

Figure 23. Lengthening of Stride

Exercise for lengthening of the stride from short (passing left), to medium to long (passing right)

Lengthening of Stride

[**Figure 23**] Extension is created by a lengthening of the horse's stride that is desired when the rider wants to cover more ground at a walk or trot than would be possible with a highly collected horse. A collected horse will direct some of its impulsion to moving upward to increase the elevation of its steps that impedes forward movement, while the extended horse directs most of its impulsion to moving forward.

Levade

Horse being trained for lengthening of stride.

A horse can be trained to lengthen its stride, and therefore extension, by placing narrow diameter posts or landscape timbers on the ground at distances just a little over a normal stride. The rider then trains for extension by trotting over the posts which forces the horse to stretch to cover the next post. In this manner the horse is forced to work the muscles of his back and loins longitudinally which later can be associated with leg and rein aids. Similarly a series of posts can be placed in a semi circle like spokes of a wheel. The rider can practice lengthening the stride by trotting over the poles furthest outward and practice shortening the stride by trotting over the posts furthest inward, alternatively lengthening and shortening the horse's stride.

Levade

[**Figure 24**] A levade is an advanced dressage movement in which the horse lowers the hindquarters, with hocks brought completely under the body, and raises the forelegs high off the ground.

Lifting Hand

With a "lifting hand" both reins are raised to correct a horse that is overly flexed or boring down on the bit. It can also correct a

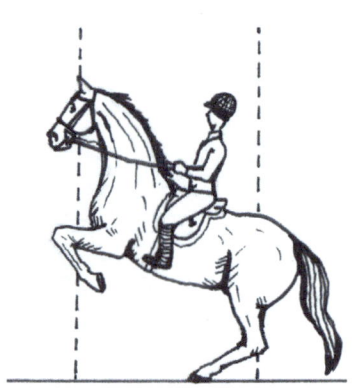

Figure 24. Levade

The Levade marked by lowering of the quarters and forehands off the ground

heavy forehand in which the horse's head hangs too low. (See also *Rein Aids*)

Lunging

[**Figure 25**] Lunging consists of exercising a horse in a circular pattern on a line approximately 35 feet in length. On command, and often with the accompaniment of a lunging *whip* pointing toward the horse's girth, the horse moves 360 degrees around the trainer at the center.

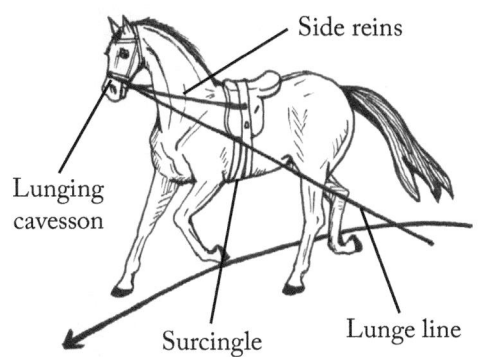

Figure 25. Lunging

Work on the lunge line with training cavesson, side reins and surcingle

In lunging the young horse, *side reins* may be used in conjunction with a lunging *cavesson* and *surcingle* to promote collection and to move the horse in a steady *cadence*. Side reins, made to exhibit elasticity, are attached to rings on each side of the lunging cavesson, which takes the place of the halter, and to the surcingle, which can replace or be placed over the saddle. Side reins attached to a surcingle, as opposed to a saddle, prevent the side reins from moving up as the reins are progressively tightened to exact more collection. As training progresses, the side reins are shortened to promote greater collection and to move the horse at a collected trot and canter.

In lunging, the horse is first shown the whip which is passed gently over and under the hindquarters. The whip is a *pushing aid* and should not be used on the hindquarters but pointed toward where the rider's legs would be. If the horse tries to come into the center of the circle, the whip should be pointed towards him so that the tip touches his nose. The surcingle, side reins, cavesson, whip, and voice are the essential tools of lunging. (See also *Cavesson and Side Reins*)

Lunging, at the canter

To begin the canter while on the lunge line, the horse is pulled slightly into the circle creating some slack in the lunge line and then encouraged to go back out onto the circle by pushing with the whip pointing at the girth. By giving some slack to the lunge line before the horse moves back out onto the circle, the horse will

Mount/dismount

Lunging at the trot with right hind and left front leg in suspension.

have more freedom to move the inside leg upward and forward to facilitate a correct transition into the canter. If the lunge line is tightened, the inside leg will have insufficient freedom to allow the horse to go into the canter.

When a young horse is on the wrong lead, whether lunging or riding, the horse should not be brought to an immediate halt, but allowed to finish the circle or trip around the arena. Stopping a young horse immediately can result in confusion, impeding the horse's willingness to go into a canter on the next command. Allow the horse to continue for a while before bringing him back to a trot and trying again. However, a schooled horse who has learned his leads should be immediately stopped when on the wrong lead, to discourage a wrong start.

Mount/dismount

To mount, the rider grasps the back of the stirrup iron with the right hand and turning it toward herself, inserts the left foot into the stirrup. The rider's left hand is then free to grasp the front of the saddle and, aided by one or two bounces on the right foot, pulls herself up and over the saddle. When losing a stirrup while riding,

Mount/dismount

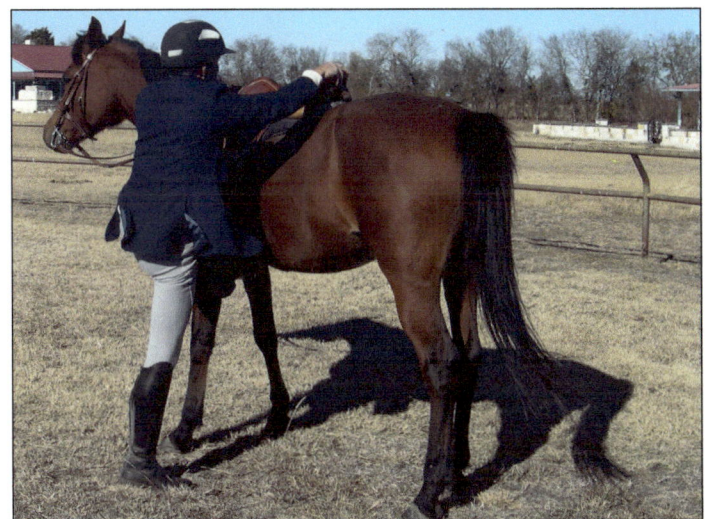

Rider in pre-mount position with right hand on the cantel and left hand holding onto the withers with reins in hand.

Rider in mounting position with forearm on the withers and reins in hand.

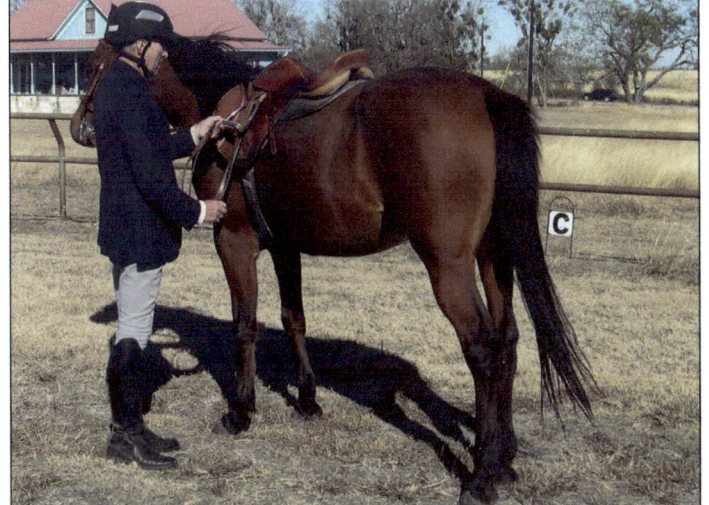

Rider at dismount pushing the stirrup up the leather and tucking the end through the stirrup.

Rider in final dismount position facing to the rear with reins in hand.

the rider should place her foot back into the stirrup by feel, rather than by looking down.

To dismount, the rider puts both reins in the left hand held taught and together and rests that hand over the neck to keep from inadvertently pulling on the reins during the dismount. Sliding the right leg over the saddle and rump of the horse, the rider steps to the ground facing the horse's side and removes her other foot from the stirrup. The rider then turns toward the rear of the horse, still holding the reins in the left hand. When not remounting, the rider slides the stirrup irons up the stirrup strap and tucks the ends through the irons.

Mounting, problems and remedies

Before mounting an anxious horse that is not standing still, move the horse forward and backward a few steps to release tension. However, a horse that doesn't stand still when being mounted is insufficiently broken. The trainer should use a rope halter with lead line and pull down whenever the horse moves accompanied with the voice command to halt. The rider should eventually practice mounting while another stands to the side (not in front) of the horse ready to pull downward on the lead line attached to a halter under the bridle whenever the horse begins to move. A rope halter will exert more pressure across the sensitive area of the nose than will a flat nylon or leather halter exacting greater obedience from the horse.

Neck Rein

See *Bearing Rein*

On the Bit

"On the bit" is when the horse has gentle contact with the bit, which is achieved when the horse is in balance and does not seek support from the reins. Being on the bit is achieved through *collection* when the horse steps under the body with its hind legs in such a way that the rider can feel a slight loosing of tension on the reins. By using leg aids to apply pressure from the sides of the horse and squeezing slightly with the hands, the rider is able to make the horse step more under the body with its hind legs and, by restraining him with the reins, cause him to round his back and raise his neck so that his crest comes nearer to the rider. The horse will then be "on the bit." (See also *Squeezing Up* and *Above and Behind the Bit*)

Pace

Pace is the speed at which the horse moves forward governed by the *gaits*, e.g., walk, trot, and canter. The horse's gait determines the sequence of steps taken. While the *gait* governs the horse's forward movement by the sequence of steps taken, the pace is the rate at which the horse moves (for example, number of yards covered per minute) which can vary considerably within a gait, thus making it possible for a horse at an extended walk to move at a faster pace than one at a collected trot.

Figure 26. Passage

The Passage marked by elevated steps with horse moving with prolonged suspension

Passage

[**Figure 26**] A passage is a slow and highly cadenced elevated trot with a long moment of suspension. The horse appears to move in slow motion, floating while moving forward, making it look as if the horse is dancing.

Passive (holding) Rein

See *Holding Rein*

Figure 27. Piaffe

The Piaffe marked by elevated steps in place

Piaffe

[**Figure 27**] The *piaffe* is a cadenced elevated trot-like movement performed in place. The horse maintains a clear and even rhythm, shows strong elevated impulsion and has a moment of suspension between the foot falls.

Pirouette

The pirouette is a 180, 270 or 360 degree turn in place at a collected walk or collected canter in which the horse makes a circle with its front end around a smaller circle made by the hind end. The front legs and outside hind leg should travel around the inside hind leg on two separate tracks, with the horse bent slightly in the direction of travel. The hind legs remain almost on the spot, but maintain the same sequence of foot placement required for the collected walk or canter. A pirouette at a walk, however, is more commonly referred to as *turning on the haunches*.

Posting

The Piaffe, illustrating the elevated trot in place during which the rider sits completely motionless in the saddle. (Photo credit: Mathias Myka)

Posting

See *Change of Diagonals* and *Gaits*

Rearing

[**Figure 28**] Rearing usually comes about when the horse refuses to move forward and wants to turn the other way. Unable to accomplish this due to the rider's application of leg aids, the horse rises up and tries to wheel around. Usually, horses rear up and to one side trying to turn around. A correction is to pull hard and intermittently on the rein opposite the direction the horse is trying to turn. The other hand and arm should be passive and leaning downward toward the horse's neck to become closer to the center of gravity which will be below the horse's neck. As the horse drops down, he should be driven forward. Rearing is one of the most serious faults in a horse due to its potential to cause injury to the rider. The correction for rearing requires an experienced rider that

Figure 28. Rearing

Correcting a rear by turning the head sharply and driving forward

Horse rearing with rider correctly displacing weight forward and moving the horse forward.

can immediately and aggressively move the horse forward by the use of leg aids.

Rein Aids

There are five basic types of rein aids:

1. Direct rein. A *direct rein* is the means by which collection or a decrease of pace is obtained. It's most important use is to straighten the horse's head and neck, with no evidence of bending or flexing to either side. The rein retains a straight line from the rider's elbow to the horse's mouth, regardless of the position of the horse's head.

2. Indirect rein. The *indirect rein* controls lateral work such as bending in a circle or shifting the horse's weight and is used

with any work where the horse must bend in the same direction it is moving. For example, a rein can be held above and slightly in front of the withers to shift the horse's weight to the opposite side just before a *flying change of lead* or a rein can be held above and behind the withers toward the rider's opposite side to shift the horse's weight from one shoulder to the opposite haunch, as in *turning on the haunches*.

3. Leading or open rein. Holding the rein out from one side of the neck for direction. A *leading rein* has no application to bending or restraining. It is used primarily in turning.

4. Neck or *bearing rein*. Directing the horse to the left or right by placing one rein against and over the neck causing the horse to turn away from the pressure and in the opposite direction.

5. Pulley rein. Pulling one rein upward and backward to execute a fast turn in an emergency that, because of its severity, should be used only to turn a horse away from danger.

Although the following are not considered types of reins, the *vibrating* and *lifting hand* can accent the direct rein as follows:

Vibrating hand. Hands alternate (see-saw) back and forth smoothly to create yield and flexion in the horse's mouth. Sometimes used to establish collection.

Lifting hand. Both reins are raised to correct a horse that is over-flexed or boring down on the bit. It can also correct a heavy forehand in which the horse's head hangs too low.

Rein-back

A rein-back is moving the horse backwards. Before reining back, the horse stands squarely on all four legs while the rider presses with both legs at the girth along with only slight tension of the reins, as if cueing the horse into a walk. At the moment the horse

Rein-back with rider slowly increasing contact with the reins while lessening contact with the legs.

is about to move forward, the horse can be made to step back by increased pressure on the reins and a lessening of contact with the legs. During initial training, a canter depart from a standstill will be easier after reining-back than from a halt, as the horse is already collected by constraining its forward movement and, therefore, is more ready to spring forward at the cue for the canter.

Rewarding the Horse

The simplest and most effective way a rider can show appreciation for a successful action is by rubbing the neck fondly and speaking with a soothing voice. Horses understand the commands of the voice more quickly than any other aid.

Rhythm

Rhythm is the regularity—or equal spacing-- of the horse's steps. The balance of a horse is best reflected by this regularity. Although sometimes confused with a horse's rhythm, a horse's *cadence* refers to the elevated (up and down) steps that a horse maintains, while

Riding with Extension

rhythm refers to the regularity or equal spacing of these steps while moving forward or in place.

Riding with Extension

Riding with extension is riding with less *flexion* in which the position of the rider is a few degrees in front of the *vertical*. Leg aids are of greater importance than use of the reins for promoting extension. Extension is achieved by lengthening the horse's stride by loosening the reins and evoking a strong forward movement with leg aids, required for hunters, dressage and a strong posting trot. (See also *Lengthening of Stride*)

Riding with the Motion

Riding with the motion is when the rider's thighs and buttocks are following the horse's movement, rather than trying to create the impulsion by pushing the horse forward. The rider's leg aids alone should be the cue for impulsion not movement of the thighs and buttocks.

Riding with extension with rider a few degrees in front of the vertical. (Photo credit: Flickr/nikki_tate)

Rollback

A rollback is a quick pivot on the haunches from either a standstill or a walk. To be able to turn quickly, the horse is made to place the bulk of its weight on the opposite hind leg from which it is turning. This is done by pulling the rein on the side to which the horse is turning toward the rider's opposite hip lightening the side to which the horse is turning. A rollback differs from a *pulley rein* in that a rollback increases the speed and tightness in which the horse is able to turn by shifting weight to the haunches creating a faster and more controlled turn-around. Rollbacks may be required in equitation classes in which the rider comes to an abrupt stop and then without hesitation turns the horse 180 degrees on its haunches.

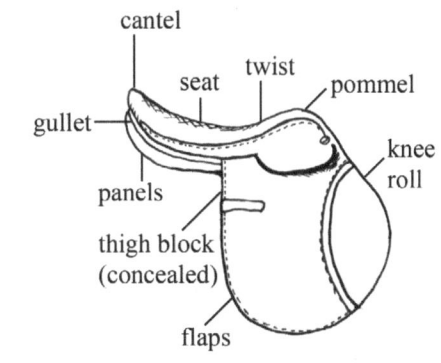

Figure 29. Saddle Language

Saddle Language

[**Figure 29**] **Cantel:** The upwardly projecting rear part of the seat of the saddle. The higher the cantle, the deeper the seat.

Gullet: The channel between the shock absorbing panels on the underside of the saddle running from front to back.

Flaps: Sides of the saddle protruding downward under the stirrup leathers. Depending on the saddle's purpose, saddle flaps may have knee rolls and padding to prevent the rider's legs from moving forward when jumping, thereby providing greater security. Some flaps are extended forward for jumping while others are positioned downward for greater cross county use and flexibility in using leg aids. Flaps also can vary in length to provide the rider more or less leg contact with the horse.

Knee rolls: Knee rolls are attached to the forward edge of the flaps or beneath them, called "hidden knee rolls," for greater security and body balance. Larger knee rolls are customary for jumping and steeple chase events to prevent the knees from moving forward during a jump.

Panels: Molded foam pads that are placed under the saddle at the sides and rear to help cushion and absorb the motion of the horse.

Saddle Types

Panels are usually smaller when more contact with the horse is desired and larger for saddles exclusively used for jumping.

Pommel: The built-up front part of the saddle. Some pommels may be "cut back" to fit better over the withers and allow the rider to move more in front of the vertical, for example, to assume a *two point position* required for equitation.

Seat: The seat of a saddle can come in various degrees of width and depth, e.g. "deep seat," to suit the rider and the event. The seats of jumping and event saddles tend to have greater depth for security; whereas the seats of show saddles tend to have less depth for closer contact with the horse and versatility of movement for cuing.

Thigh blocks: Thigh blocks represent padding toward the rear and underside of the flap that helps hold the thigh in position for greater security.

Tree: The wood, laminated or composite foundation on which the saddle is built. Trees come with various guarantees that may vary up to a "lifetime." Some also come in narrow, medium and wide trees that can be chosen to better fit the weight and frame of the horse. Generally, the lower the withers, the wider the saddle needs to be in order not to slide from side to side. A maximum of between two and three fingers, positioned vertically, should fit between the withers and the underside of the saddle at the pommel for the proper saddle width.

Twist: The width of saddle seat just below the pommel at the crotch of the rider, chosen in accord with the weight and frame of the rider. A narrow twist provides more contact with the horse, allowing more of the rider's thighs to be in contact with the horse.

Saddle Types

All Purpose: Designed for maximum versatility riding on the flat and over low jumps. They are characterized by small knee rolls for

Close contact saddle illustrating smaller flaps and narrower twist for increased thigh and leg contact.

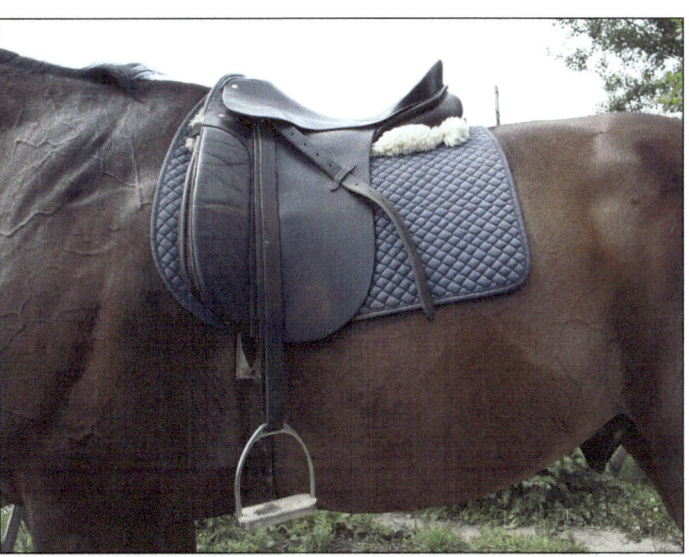

Dressage saddle illustrating the vertical position of the flaps, allowing for more flexible cueing.

light jumping, flaps that are less forward than a true jumping saddle to accommodate flat work, and a deeper seat for security.

Close Contact: Designed for jumping as well as riding on the flat with the maximum of rider contact with the horse and thereby sensitivity of the horse to seat and leg aids. They are characterized by a narrower *twist* (See *Saddle Language*) and a smaller "sweat" flap beneath the outer flap allowing the rider's legs to be more in contact with the horse with the smallest possible gap between flap and thigh.

Dressage: Designed exclusively for dressage and riding on the flat. They are characterized by flaps positioned vertically rather than forward to support a greater variety of leg aids.

Equitation: Designed exclusively for equitation in which the form and balance of the rider is being judged. Although similar to other types of saddles, the equitation saddle may be characterized by a lower pommel to allow the two point position required in equitation and better weight distribution to keep the rider balanced.

Seat and Posture, correct

Event: Designed for the combined performances of dressage, endurance, and jumping in which the same saddle is used for all three events. They are characterized by incorporating the requirements for dressage (flexibility), endurance (comfort) and jumping (security) in the same saddle with the least compromise.

Jumping: Designed exclusively for jumping. Characterized by forward flaps, substantial knee rolls and lower pommel so that the rider can more easily assume a forward position over the jump. Most incorporate thigh blocks beneath and to the rear of the flaps to help keep the rider's legs in the correct position.

Show (seat): Designed primarily for Park and English and Country Pleasure in which the rider is positioned back as far as possible to lighten the horse for greater elevation of the forelegs. Characterized by a low cut back pommel, a wide nearly flat seat and vertically positioned flaps to allow greater freedom of movement.

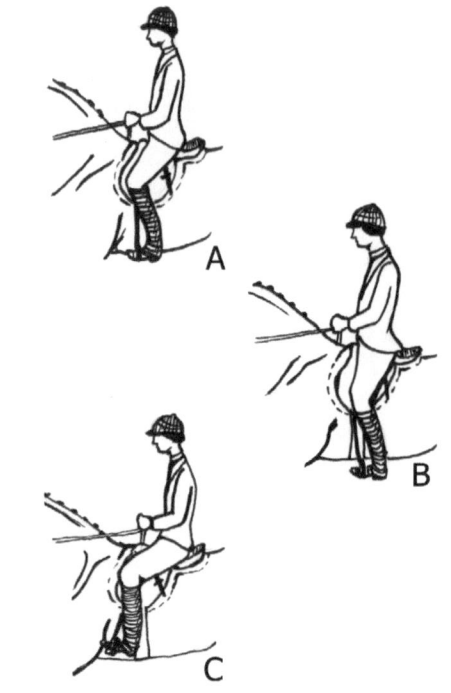

Figure 30. Seat and Posture, correct

(A) Correct seat: Shoulders back and chest arched outward; (B) Fork seat: Hips forward and legs behind the rider; (C) Chair seat: Legs forward and rider sitting at the back of the saddle

Seat and Posture, correct

[**Figure 30**] The correct "seat" and riding posture is exhibited by the following:

Back and body: The rider's back is upright and braced with a slight upward push just above the buttocks. At the canter, the rider's body is only a few degrees in front of the vertical. At the posting trot the rider is no more than 20 degrees in front of the vertical.

Eyes: The rider should be looking forward over the ears of the horse. Eyes, not head, glance downward to check for the correct lead.

Forearms, wrists and hands: The forearms and wrists are pointing forward with thumbs four inches apart. Hands are over and slightly in front of the withers.

Seat and Posture, correct

Head and neck: The rider's head and neck follow a straight line that runs from the head through the upper body down to the heels.

Heels: Heels are pointing slightly down to maintain proper distribution of the rider's weight making them the lowest point of the rider.

Knees: Knees are against the saddle with the least possible gap between knee and flap.

Legs: The lower legs hang close to the horse's body at the position of the girth.

Shoulders: The rider's shoulders are back, flattened against the back, and chest arched outward from the body. Both shoulders are in alignment so that a line drawn through them forms a right angle to the spine of the horse. The rider should be sitting upright but not stiff and be relaxed without slouching (Figure 30A). To be avoided are hips forward of the vertical and legs behind the

Rider illustrating the proper heels down position.

Rider with head, elbows and heels in correct alignment.

Serpentine, at trot and canter

vertical, called a "fork seat" (Figure 30B). Also to be avoided are legs pushed forward of the vertical and chest and head behind the vertical, called a "chair seat" (Figure 30C).

Thighs and buttocks: The rider's thighs are turned inwards from the hip to firmly touch the saddle. At the walk the rider's thighs and buttocks are moving with the horse, not pushing. At the walk and sitting trot the rider's crotch absorbs the up and down motion of the horse, but at the canter, the buttocks and thighs absorb the shock. Thighs and buttocks are sunk into the saddle as deeply as possible, so that the rider's buttocks do not move forward and backward. The horse and rider should appear as one.

Serpentine, at trot and canter

[**Figure 31**] The serpentine is a dressage pattern and exercise in which the rider in a posting trot or canter bends the horse in the direction of travel around each of three (or more) loops and, before changing diagonals or leads, straightens the horse for a few steps as it approaches, crosses, and departs the *centerline*. The rider's shoulder should be directly above the centerline when changing diagonals or leads. The rider halts over the centerline at the end of the arena to complete the serpentine.

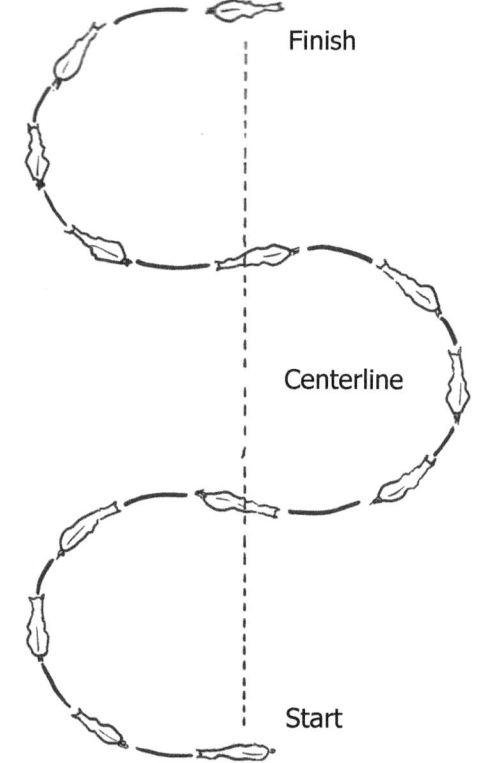

Figure 31. Serpentine, at trot and canter

Three loop serpentine showing correct bend in the loops and straightness over the center line

Setting the Head

[**Figure 32**] Setting the horse's head is a process whereby with slight pressure from the legs and a gentle squeezing of the hands, the horse's head is moved toward the vertical and the horse's neck becomes bowed, at which time the horse "moves into the bit" and becomes collected. (See also *Squeezing Up*)

Shoulder-in at Halt, Walk and Trot

[**Figure 33**] Shoulder-in at a halt is when one of the horse's front legs is behind the other while standing and the horse is slightly bent around the rider's opposite leg. To shoulder-in on the right standing, the rider uses a right indirect rein and right leg aid a hand behind the girth. The right leg aid moves the haunches

Figure 32. Setting the Head

Setting the horse's head at halt with some flexion and movement toward the vertical

slightly to the left, while, simultaneously, the right indirect rein drawn toward the rider moves the horse back one step. The horse's right foreleg will then be positioned behind the left foreleg standing.

When right shoulder-in is performed at a walk or trot, the rider's right leg a hand behind the girth moves the haunches to the left and cues the horse forward pushing the horse with an up and down ankle to calf to knee movement into two slightly different tracts, an inside tract for the forelegs and an outside tract for the hind legs. A *left holding* leg restricts the movement of the hindquarters outward while a right indirect rein slightly to the right completes the bend. When right shoulder-in is performed at a walk or trot, the horse's left foreleg passes and crosses in front of the right foreleg while the horse is looking away from the direction of movement at about a 30 degree angle from the track. This distinguishes it from *haunches out*, which requires the horse to be looking forward, in the direction of movement. Shoulder-in is required preparation for more advanced movements because the horse must place one of its hind legs beneath its body and place it in front of the other hind leg lightening and collecting the horse.

» *Quick Cue Note:* Right shoulder-in at halt. Right indirect rein drawn slightly back and right leg a hand behind girth pushing with an up and down ankle to calf to knee movement. Right shoulder-in at a walk or trot. From a walk or trot, the right leg moves the haunches to the left and cues the horse to move forward pushing the horse into two slightly different tracks. A left holding leg restricts movement of the haunches outward and a right indirect rein keeps the head about 30 degrees to the right.

Shying

[**Figure 34**] Shying occurs when the horse becomes startled and quickly moves away from an unfamiliar object. It involves moving sideways, rather than forward, usually for only a second or two. Although normally corrected with age and experience, shying can

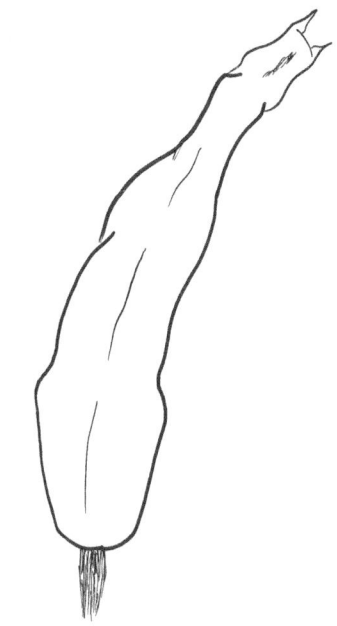

Figure 33. Shoulder-in at Halt, Walk, Trot

Right shoulder-in with head at 30° angle and right shoulder behind the left shoulder

Figure 34. Shying

Correcting a shy with an indirect rein on the side away from the cause of fright

Side Pass, half and true

be checked during or immediately afterward by several momentary upward actions with an indirect rein in the direction opposite in which the horse is shying. A horse that consistently shies should not be ridden with slack reins, so that the bit is always in gentle contact with the mouth to quickly check the shying.

Side Pass, half and true

[**Figure 35**] The side pass is a combination of leg and rein aids. It is an important movement in that it provides the practice for the change of leads at the canter and more advanced movements in dressage. In a half-pass the horse moves at a walk forward and sideways at the same time, so that the horse's front and rear legs are on different tracks, while the head remains straight ahead. In a true side pass the horse's forward movement is restrained to practically a standstill while moving sideways on parallel tracks.

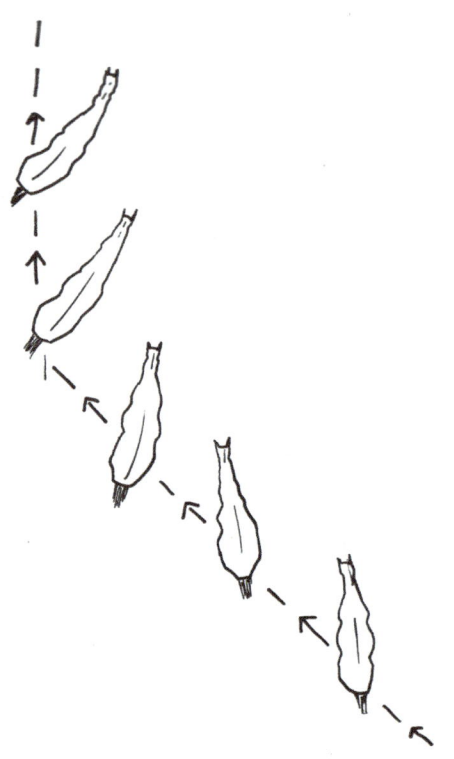

Figure 35. Side Pass, half and true

Half-pass and then side pass

Half-pass to the left with right legs crossing in front of left leg while moving to the side and forward at the same time.

Side Pass, half and true

The rider begins teaching the half-pass by shortening the reins to flex and collect the horse. For a right to left half-pass, the rider uses a left indirect rein to shift the horse's weight to the right and lighten the horse on the side to which it will be moving. This rein will also have the effect of keeping the horse's head and neck straight while moving sideways. The rider simultaneously applies the right leg just behind the girth in an undulating (up and down) motion from ankle to calf to knee to move the horse to the left. The alternating pressure from ankle to calf to knee encourages the horse to move sideways. Soon the rider can merge the pressure of the ankle, calve, and knee into one simultaneous action. The left indirect rein can alternate with a leading rein to regulate the speed and amount of lateral shift and limit the forward movement. The left leg at the girth is used to encourage forward motion. Now the horse will be moving forward and sideways at the same time. This will produce the half-pass.

» *Quick Cue Note:* Half-pass left. Collect, right ankle to calf to knee action to create sideways movement, left leg at girth to encourage forward movement, left indirect rein to keep head forward and regulate forward speed.

After the horse is working at the half-pass you can practice the true side pass. In a true side pass the horse's forward movement is restrained to practically a standstill. The right leg behind the girth continues its undulating motion but the left leg now remains passive and is no longer used to move the horse forward. When the horse begins to move left, use the left rein to keep the head straight and to slowly curtail forward movement. If needed use a crop lightly on the right haunch to encourage the horse to move sideways. Now, you are going slightly forward and sideways at the same time with a rocking motion with more sideways than forward movement. With practice the forward movement can be curtailed to a standstill.

Side Reins

» *Quick Cue Note:* True side pass left. Collect, right ankle to calf to knee action to create sideways movement, left indirect rein to keep head forward and impede forward movement.

Side Reins

[Figure 36] Side reins are usually attached to a lunging *cavesson* and *surcingle* during lunging exercises in which the trainer wishes to promote collection in a young horse in small steps. This is accomplished by tightening the side reins a slight amount once every other training session or so until the horse's head is slightly in front of the vertical. The same effect may be attained with a snaffle bit and bridle in which the reins are tied around the horn of a western saddle and slowly tightened over a period of lunge line training. However, this method requires the use of a bit at an early age and as the reins are tightened to promote collection at the canter, the saddle may move forward, loosening the side reins. The trainer relieves all tension on the side reins for the first few lunging sessions and only tightens them gradually thereafter. (See also *Lunging*)

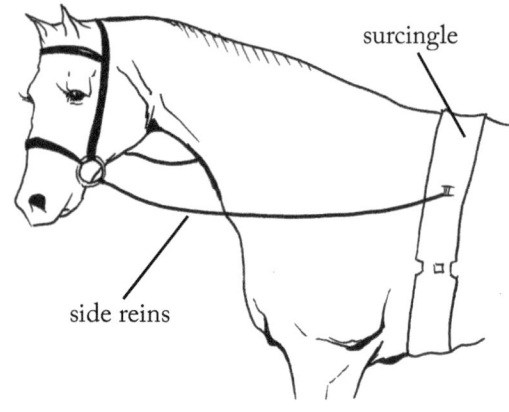

Figure 36. Side Reins
Side reins attached to surcingle

Sitting Trot

A sitting trot is when the rider is sitting in the saddle as opposed to "posting," in which the rider should be up in the saddle when the horse's left (outside) front leg is in the air in the clockwise direction and up in the saddle when the horse's right (outside) front leg is in the air in the counter clockwise direction. (See also *Change of Diagonals*)

Snaffle Bit

The snaffle is popular bit for training that is "broken" or jointed in the middle with "O" or "D" rings on either side to which reins are attached. When the reins are shortened the snaffle bit places pressure on the tongue encouraging the horse to move the head back placing more weight on the hind legs than on the forelegs. Early training focuses on encouraging the horse to work from the hind legs in preparation for more complex commands that require

Inside the Grand Arena of the Spanish Riding School, Vienna, Austria. (Photo credit: Flickr/davidharding)

impulsion from behind and the redistribution of weight to the haunches. (See also *Bitting*)

Spanish Riding School (Spanische Hofreitschule)

Although the roots of the Spanish Riding School can be traced to 1572, its "modern" day beginning dates to 1729 in Vienna, Austria, when Emperor Charles the VI gave the order to build a riding hall to provide a dignified home for the special art of training horses that had already become known as the Spanish Riding School. To

Spurs, correct use of

this day, in accordance with protocol, every rider on entering the great hall salutes the portrait of Emperor Charles the VI, symbolizing a gratitude to him for building the facility (a tradition that is carried on today in tests of dressage). The classical principles of horsemanship which the Spanish Riding School emulates represents over 400 years of training and riding etiquette and instruction which is kept to this day by the rules and protocol of the Spanish Riding School. Many current day styles of riding, most notably dressage, borrow heavily on the principles and techniques of the Spanish Riding School as do many books that instruct new riders. Although situated in the heart of Austria, the Spanish Riding School acquired its name by training almost exclusively horses sent to it by the king of Spain, and has kept that name ever since.

Spurs, correct use of

Spurs are attached to the heels of the rider's boots for the purpose of heightening the effect of the leg aids used in training. After the horse has been taught to respond to natural leg aids, spurs are sometimes used to sharpen the horse's responsiveness to commands, just as a whip or crop may be used to focus the horse's attention and move the horse more quickly into an upward transition. However, spurs should not be used at the early stages of training when they can have the effect of causing the horse to overreact, confusing the horse and making training more difficult. The use of spurs can range from a brief, light touch to encourage more impulsion to greater pressure when a horse refuses to go forward. There are many types of spurs that are divided between Western and English riding. English riders exclusively use spurs with short stubby shanks of about a half inch to three quarters of an inch long curved slightly downward so as to lighten the effect on the horse. Western spurs often have small wheels attached to shanks that can be rotated with the rider's leg action to create a stronger effect. Depending on the horse, spurs can be an aid to training and riding but they are not a requirement for good horsemanship.

Spur (½–¾") in correct heals down position.

Squeezing Up

"Squeezing up" is an expression for moving the horse into the bit to collect the horse. It involves gently squeezing the hands to increase tension on the reins, and simultaneously applying pressure from the legs, from which the horse becomes collected with hind legs and forelegs moving under the horse and neck flexed. Squeezing up readies the horse for making upward transitions, for example, from a halt to a canter, since the horse, without any forward motion for propulsion, must "spring" into the canter from the resulting energy "collected" between the horse's forelegs and hind legs as a result of squeezing up.

Stirrups, drop and pickup

Whether in the heat of making a transition in the arena or dealing with a startled horse on the trail, a rider may inadvertently drop a foot out of a stirrup. Therefore, dropping and picking up a stirrup is a necessary training exercise and a test of good equitation skills. Since showmanship and maintaining good balance may require the use of feel rather than vision, picking up a dropped stirrup is properly executed with the rider looking forward the entire time. Dropping both feet out of the stirrups, the rider can tell where the stirrups are by feeling where they hit in relation to her ankle. With this cue, she inserts her feet into the stirrups without dropping her eyes to look. This should be practiced by every beginning rider.

Stirrups, riding without

Riding without stirrups on a well-schooled horse is an effective exercise for learning proper balance, as without the support of stirrups the body naturally finds the proper position and weight distribution for comfort in riding. After mounting, the exercise consists of the rider picking up each stirrup and crossing it over to the other side just in front of the saddle, tucking the stirrup leathers under the edge of the flaps of the saddle if possible to steady them during posting. The rider shows no change in position when the stirrups are removed and appears as stable and effective as with stirrups. The leg should be in the same position as with stirrups,

Riding without stirrups, for practicing proper balance.

with the heel of the foot retaining its downward and forward angular appearance.

Surcingle

A surcingle is a training device used during lunging that takes the place of the saddle to which is attached *side reins* for the purpose of teaching collection during the early stages of training. The surcingle, depending on type, may be attached over the saddle or directly to the horse. The advantage of the surcingle is that, unlike side reins that are sometimes attached to the side of a Western saddle to teach collection during lunging, the surcingle tends to remain stationary and not move forward when the side reins are increasingly tightened to encourage greater collection. The surcingle is usually used together with a lunging *cavesson*—an abbreviated halter with a band around the midpoint of the nose with rings on the sides and top to which are connected the side reins and a lunge line. (See also *Side Reins*)

Suspension

Suspension is the amount of spring developed from the hindquarters which produces a strong carrying and pushing force. Large amounts of suspension can create a highly elevated trot. A movement in dressage that requires a high degree of suspension is the *passage*. It is a slow and highly *cadenced* (elevated) trot with a long moment of suspension, in which the horse appears to move in slow motion.

Top Line

See *Croup*

Transitions

In a correct downward transition, the rider braces her back, applies pressure with the legs to engage the hocks, and shifts weight from the stirrups to the saddle, thereby lowering the horse's quarters. In an upward transition the rider collects the horse by using leg pressure to engage the hocks at the same time gently squeezing the hands to place a slight tension on the reins. This "collects" energy between the forelegs and hind legs which, when cued, provides the momentum needed for the upward transition.

Figure 37. Trot

(A) Working trot, more extension and less elevation; (B) Collected trot, more elevation and less extension

Trot (working, collected, extended)

[**Figure 37**] The trot is a distinct *gait* of which there are at least three different types. The difference between the various trots—the working (normal or medium) trot, the collected trot, and the extended trot—does not lie so much in the acceleration or the reduction of the speed of the horse, as it does with the lengthening of the stride or the distance the forelegs are reaching out while maintaining the same *rhythm*. The length of stride for the collected trot is between the working trot and the extended trot, with the most distance traveled per minute being covered with the extended trot and least with the working trot. A sitting trot is usually a slow to medium pace used in conjunction with a working trot, in which the rider's weight is sunk into the saddle (not posting) and the rider is positioned no more than just a few degrees in front of the *vertical*.

In a trot the horse moves in a two beat rhythm in which the right rear and left front leg hit the ground together, followed a moment

Trot (working, collected, extended)

later by the left rear and right front leg together with a brief moment of suspension between in which all four legs are off the ground. In the trot the horse carries his own and his rider's weight with the two diagonal legs. The regular hoof beats of the diagonal legs, interrupted by the moment of suspension, give the rhythm of the movement. The shortening of the stride at the same rhythm will require the legs to be raised higher. These lively, elevated steps are known as *cadence*.

A *working trot* is a pace in which a horse is not collected but shows proper balance, is on the bit, and moves forward with even elastic steps. The rider may be sitting or posting. With small variations this is also called a normal or medium trot.

Working (normal) trot marked by less collection and elevation with head in front of the vertical.

A *collected trot* is a pace in which a horse's head is at or near the vertical and hocks and forelegs under the body of the horse with neck bowed. The rider usually posts to a collected trot, also called a "rising trot".

An *extended trot* is a pace in which the horse's stride lengthens with the forelegs reaching in front of the body but the hocks remain

Trot (working, collected, extended)

The collected trot marked by a shortening of stride and greater flexion.

The extended trot marked by the lengthening of stride or distance the forelegs are reaching out while maintaining the same rhythm.

under the body to maintain the impulsion needed to drive the horse forward, with more weight on the hind legs than the forelegs. The rider may be sitting or posting. (See also *Extension*)

Work at a trot remains the foundation of the training of a horse, because it is best suited for obtaining and preserving impulsion,

Turn/half-turn on Forehand at Halt

while improving suppleness and obedience. The rider can influence her horse better in the trot than at the walk, where natural impulsion is lacking, or in the canter where the horse can rapidly change the level of impulsion and imbalance the rider.

To produce a collected trot, use the legs while preventing fast forward movement with *half halts* to collect the horse and encourage the horse to step higher rather than further. The resulting energy that would be used to go forward will now be used to raise the legs in an elevated trot.

Turn/half-turn on Forehand at Halt

[**Figure 38**] Turn on the forehand at halt is executed with lateral (same side) aids. While the horse is at a halt, the horse's neck is bent in the direction of the turn with an inside indirect rein drawn low toward the rider's opposite hip. The rider's inside leg is drawn back a hand behind the girth in order to activate the haunches into sideways movement.

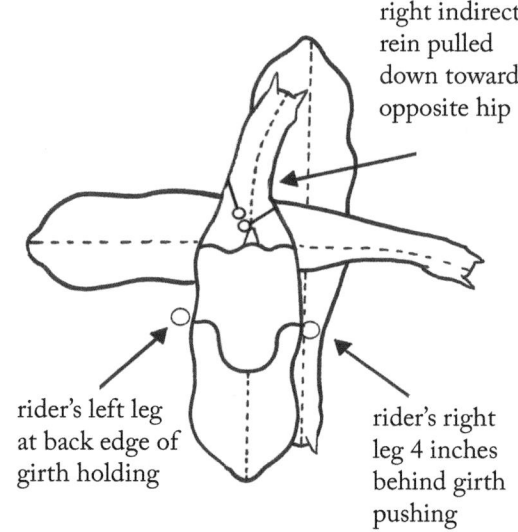

Figure 38. Turn/half-turn on Forehand at Halt

Turning on the forehand to the right

While the rider's inside rein maintains the bend in the neck and the inside leg pushes the haunches in the direction of the turn, the opposite rein and leg just behind the girth holds the horse from stepping forward or sideways. The horse's steps should be cadenced, with inside foreleg stepping in place, the outside foreleg stepping around the inside foreleg, and the inside hind leg crossing the outside hind leg. Turning left or right on the forelegs is a continuation of left or right *shoulder-in* at halt where the rider now continually applies lateral leg and indirect rein aids to move the horse completely around.

» ***Quick Cue Note:*** Turn on the forehand. Inside indirect rein drawn low toward rider's opposite hip, then, inside leg a hand behind the girth pushing and outside rein and leg just behind the girth holding.

Turn/half-turn on Haunches at Halt

Horse beginning to turn on the forehand to the left. (Photo credit: Flickr/ Gillian Clancy)

Turn/half-turn on Haunches at Halt

[**Figure 39**] Turning on the haunches is a movement from the halt or medium walk in which the horse pivots on the inside hind leg, bent in the direction of the turn.

Although there are several approaches to turning on the haunches, to begin, the rider should bend the horse's neck slightly in the direction of the turn with an *indirect rein* placed farther to the inside (in the direction of the turn) then the normal indirect rein position. This inside rein at first acts as a subtle *leading rein* while the outside rein restricts forward movement and later can be used as a *neck rein* to assist in the turn. As the horse begins to turn, the inside rein that had been used as a subtle leading rein is drawn back and high toward the rider's opposite side at the level of the rider's chest to shift the horse's weight from forehand to haunches. Then, exerting pressure with an inside leg placed a hand behind the girth, the rider begins to move the horse's haunches while assisting

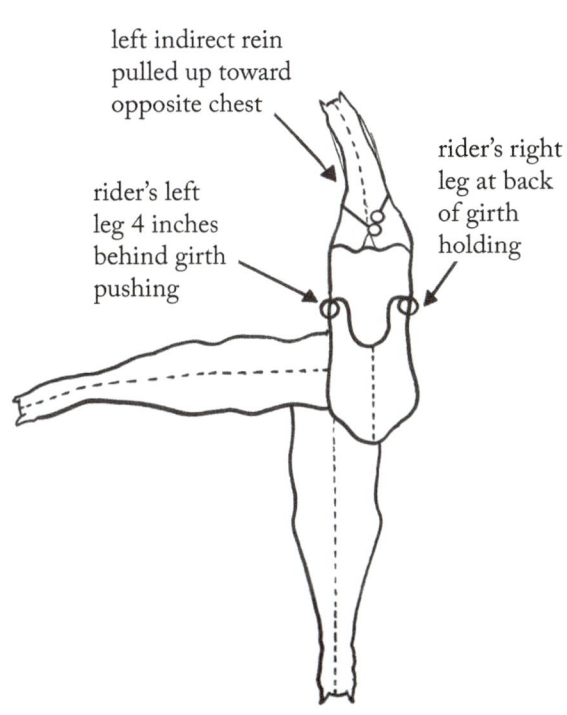

Figure 39. Turn/half-turn on Haunches at Halt

Turning on the haunches to the left

Two and Three-point Position

the turn, if necessary, with an outside neck rein, causing the inside hind leg to cross its outside hind leg in the rhythm of the walk. The rider's outside leg provides pressure to hold the horse from moving to the outside causing the horse to pivot around the inside leg.

While moving in a small circle during the turn on the haunches, the horse should remain bent from head to tail in the direction of the turn. The combination of the rider's outside leg (placed behind the girth) holding the horse and the rider's inside leg (placed a hand behind the girth) lightly pushing causes the horse to be bent from head to tail as the horse steps around the turn.

» *Quick Cue Note:* Turn on haunches. Inside indirect rein drawn high to the opposite side of the rider's chest, outside bearing (neck) rein, inside pushing leg a hand behind girth and outside leg holding just behind the girth.

Figure 40. Two-point Position

Two-point position in which rider leans slightly forward and up out of the saddle.

Two and Three-point Position

[**Figure 40**] Two and three point positions refer to different positions of weight distribution. Two point contact lifts the rider's weight off the horse's back and puts it onto the rider's heels and stirrups. The body, by leaning slightly forward, and slightly up out of the seat of the saddle lightens the horse's back and allows the balance of weight to shift forward. The two points of contact between horse and rider are the rider's legs, hence two-point position. When working and jumping at fast paces, a two-point contact is required to maintain balance which would be diminished by continual contact with the seat of the saddle, and, therefore, is the position used in jumping, cross-country galloping, and in hunt seat equitation.

The three point contact is used for most riding situations. A three-point position is distinguished by contact between the horse and rider at the seat as well as both legs, hence, three points of contact. However, the rider's seat bones not the buttocks support the rider most of the time. In the three-point position, the rider is inclined

Two and Three-point Position

Rider in two-point position in which the rider's seat is off the saddle with the feet making two points of contact.

forward, in front of the vertical, in the faster gates, such as a posting trot, canter and gallop. However, the rider is considerably more in front of the *vertical* (about 20 degrees) at the posting trot than in the canter and gallop (about 2 degrees) and at or slightly in front of the vertical at the walk and working trot.

In tests of hunter equitation, the rider assumes both a three point and two point position. The rider begins the upward transition into the canter in the first corner of the arena from a "three-point position"—the two legs and seat making three points of contact with the horse while the upper body is inclined about 2 to 3 degrees in front of the vertical. At the first corner the rider begins the upward transition to a canter by (a) shifting weight onto the outside stirrup, (b) using a slight indirect inside rein to move the horse's head toward the rail, and (c) cueing with the outside leg just behind the girth assuming a two-point position with the upper body about 20 degrees in front of the vertical. The rider increases the pace to a hand gallop approaching the second corner, increasing the horse's speed and maintaining 20 degrees in front of vertical down the side of the ring. The rider then returns to a three-point position prior to a halt.

Two Tracking

[**Figure 41**] Two tracking is when the horse is moving forward with front legs on one track while the hind legs are on another track. Training a horse to two track (for example, in *haunches-in* and *haunches-out*) can precede the canter depart as an aid to helping the horse depart on the correct lead and plays a central role in several dressage movements. A horse can be placed on two tracks by pushing the horse's haunches to one side (either haunches-in or haunches-out) at a walk or trot with an undulating ankle to calf to knee movement a hand behind the girth and an indirect rein on the opposite side to lighten the horse in the direction of movement, creating a half-pass. The horse will be walking or trotting on two tracks, the front legs following a track inside or outside that followed by the hind legs, depending on whether the haunches are positioned toward the inside or outside. In dressage, *haunches-in* is a movement that requires two tracking. Haunches-in is a lateral movement in which the horse two tacks with head parallel to the rail. The horse's hind legs are inside the track while the front legs are on the tract and the horse's neck and head are forward, in the direction of movement. Two tracking can be accomplished with the same leg and rein aids used for the *half-pass* at a walk or trot. (See also *Haunches-in/out*)

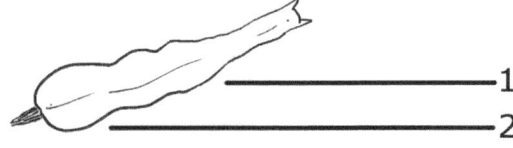

Figure 41. Two Tracking

Two tracking as used in shoulders-in, half-pass, and haunches-in/out

Unilateral Half-halt

A unilateral half-halt is frequently used in preparing a horse for a transition by shifting the horse's weight to the opposite side with an *indirect rein*. To execute a unilateral half-halt, one rein is momentarily pulled and released in several actions above and in front of the withers just prior to cueing.

For example, a unilateral half-halt may be used in changing leads at the center of a figure eight pattern to lighten the horse on the side to which the new lead will be taken. In changing from the right to the left lead at the center, a unilateral half halt with the left indirect rein shifts the horse's weight to the right side lightening the left for the change to the new lead.

The Vertical

[**Figure 42**] The "vertical" is an imaginary line drawn perpendicular from the ground to the head of the horse. When the horse is "on the vertical" the head will be tucked back and nose pointing downward parallel to an imaginary vertical line perpendicular to the ground. The horse's head can also be "behind the vertical" in which case the horse may be overly collected and forward movement is being impaired. Or, the horse's head can be "in front of the vertical" in which case the horse is less collected and more extended. In extreme cases in which the horse is far in front of the vertical the rider may lose control of the horse that is leaning on the reins and too extended. (See also *Above and Behind the Bit*)

Figure 42. The Vertical
Horse at the vertical with head tucked back and nose down.

Voice Commands

Voice commands are the simplest and most effective way a rider can show appreciation for a successful action or reinforce a command at the initial stages of training, such as "halt," "walk," and "slow." A horse understands the commands of the voice more quickly than any other aid.

Volte

[**Figure 43**] A small circle, six meters (19.5 ft) in diameter used in dressage exercises and tests. Its purpose is to train for suppleness in bending in each direction.

Figure 43. Volte
Volte for training suppleness in bending

Weight, rider's as an aid

A redistribution of the rider's weight often accompanies an upward or downward transition. For example, in transitioning upward from a trot to a canter the rider shifts weight to the back and slightly to the side opposite the desired lead prior to the cue in order to help lighten the horse on the side to which the horse will begin to lead. In transitioning downward from a trot to a walk, the rider redistributes weight by releasing the pressure normally placed downward on the stirrups and allowing the buttocks to fall more firmly into the saddle, which itself should constitute the cue to transition from a canter to a walk and a trot to a walk.

Whips

Whips

[**Figure 44**] Although there are many styles and sizes of whips, also called "bats." "crops," "quirts," and "sticks," four sizes, each with its own purpose, are commonly used. The shortest is the bat, about 18–24 inches, that may include a leather band on the handle into which the rider slips a wrist to prevent its loss. The bat is used for correcting the horse by light taps on the neck, as its short length prevents using it to the rear of the horse without a loss in balance. A second whip called a crop, about 26 to 36 inches in length, is used for that purpose. In both cases, bats and crops are held pointing behind the rider until needed. A third, longer "whip" is used for showing in halter classes to assist in moving the horse into proper position for judging. This whip, about 48 inches in length, is held above the horse's head pointed behind the trainer until needed to check the horse's forward movement when pulling gently on the lead to "stretch out" the horse's neck and to achieve *flexion*. A fourth class of whips is used in lunging a horse. These whips are approximately 6 feet in length with another six feet of tassel that can be held alongside the whip or left to fall to the ground when not in use to create a longer reach. This whip is used to follow the horse at the girth during lunging to encourage a proper pace and for pointing at the horse's nose to check the horse when cutting inward reducing the pattern. It generally is not used in contact with the horse.

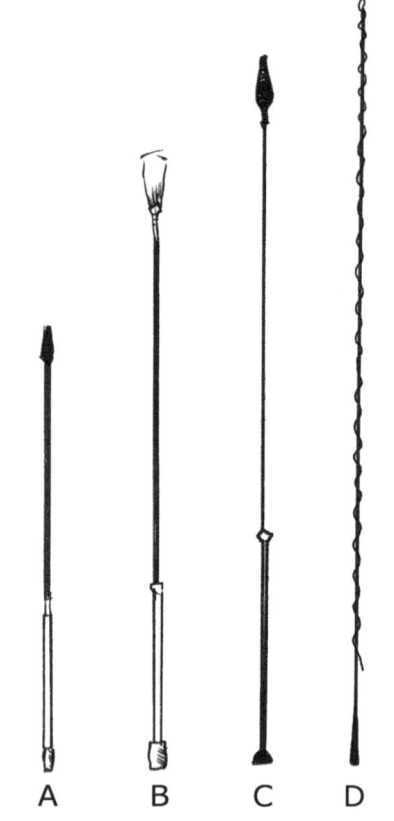

Figure 44. Whips
(A) Bat
(B) Crop
(C) Halter show whip,
(D) Lunging whip

Yielding Rein

A yielding rein is a rein aid that is applied to maintain a slight tension on the horse when a required movement of the opposite rein would ordinarily cause it to be tightened. A yielding rein moves as required, but keeps slight tension on bit or neck. For example, in riding in a circle the inside rein supported by a yielding outside rein bends the neck in the direction of travel. The outside yielding rein, must loosen (yield) to the same extent that the inside rein tightens to keep the horse bent in the direction of travel.

Zenophon

[**Spelled Xenophon**] The author of one of the earliest books on horsemanship, *De Re Equestri* (*On the Art of Horsemanship*), written by an eloquent and articulate Greek statesman and general, Xenophon, circa 350 BCE. This 12 chapter book covering everything from "Breaking the Colt," to "Advanced Training" has impressed even modern day trainers by its preciseness of explanations and by the author's insights into the feelings of the horse. Xenophon's training techniques were based on common sense and kind treatment that are followed by riding masters today. You can read about this master horseman in Xenophon, The Art of Horsemanship published by CreateSpace, 2009, available at *www.amazon.com*.

Appendix A:
List of Quick Cue Notes

Bending in a circle.. 12
Inside indirect rein, inside leg pushing just behind the girth, outside holding leg a hand behind the girth.

Bending in corner 12
Outside indirect rein, inside leg pushing a hand behind the girth.

Canter depart: method (a)...17
Outside leading rein and outside leg just behind the girth to cue the horse.

Canter depart method (b) 17
Inside indirect rein to move the head to the outside, outside leg just behind the girth to cue.

Canter depart method (c)... 18
Inside indirect rein to shift the horse's weight to the outside, outside holding rein and holding leg, inside leg to cue the horse.

Change of diagonals 24
Clockwise, outside (left) front leg up, seat up. Counterclockwise, outside (right) front leg up, seat up.

Haunches-in clockwise.. 43
Left leg a hand behind the girth pushing and driving, right indirect rein to position the head forward and right leg at the girth holding to maintain the bend. Haunches-out clockwise. Right leg a hand

List of Quick Cue Notes

behind the girth pushing and driving, left indirect rein to position the head forward and left leg at the girth holding.

Right shoulder-in at halt 67
Right indirect rein drawn slightly back and right leg a hand behind girth pushing. Right shoulder-in at a walk or trot. From a walk or trot, the right leg moves the haunches to the left and cues the horse to move forward pushing the horse into two slightly different tracks. A left holding leg restricts movement of the haunches outward and a right indirect rein keeps the head about 30 degrees to the right.

Half-pass left 69
Collect, right ankle to calf to knee action to create sideways movement, left leg at girth to encourage forward movement, left indirect rein to keep head forward and regulate forward speed.

True side pass left 70
Collect, right ankle to calf to knee action to create sideways movement, left indirect rein to keep head forward and impede forward movement.

Turn on the forehand 78
Inside indirect rein drawn low toward rider's opposite hip, then, inside leg a hand behind the girth pushing and outside rein and leg just behind the girth holding.

Turn on haunches 80
Inside indirect rein drawn high to the opposite side of the rider's chest, outside bearing (neck) rein, inside pushing leg a hand behind girth and outside leg holding just behind the girth.

Appendix B:
Eighteen Essential Movements to Good Riding

Use this sheet as a checklist to record your progress in executing eighteen essential movement to good riding.

Horse _____   Rider _____

	Haven't tried it	Working on it	Some progress	Almost there	Have it nailed
Beginning					
1. Backing (rein-back)					
2. Drop and pick up stirrups					
3. Ride without stirrups					
4. Shoulder-in					
5. Turn on the forehand at halt					
6. Turn on the haunches at halt					
7. Yield left and right					
Intermediate					
8. Change diagonals (figure eight, serpentine, volte)					
9. Lengthening of stride at trot					
10. Extended walk allowing horse to stretch forward and downward					
11. Turn on the haunches after stop					
12. Haunches in at walk and trot (Travers)					
13. Two point position (trot and canter)					
14. Simple change of leads (transition from trot, one to three steps)					
Advanced					
15. Side pass and half side pass					
16. Serpentine canter with change of leads					
17. Flying change of lead every fourth stride					
18. Counter-canter					

www.ingramcontent.com/pod-product-compliance
Lightning Source LLC
Chambersburg PA
CBHW041153290426
44108CB00002B/50